W9-BCC-860

The Leader

The Leader

Developing the Skills
& Personal Qualities
You Need to Lead Effectively

Normand L. Frigon, Sr. & Harry K. Jackson, Jr.

amacom

American Management Association

New York • Atlanta • Boston • Chicago • Kansas City • San Francisco • Washington, D.C.
Brussels • Mexico City • Tokyo • Toronto

This publication is designed to provide accurate and authoritative information in regard to the subject matter covered. It is sold with the understanding that the publisher is not engaged in rendering legal, accounting, or other professional service. If legal advice or other expert assistance is required, the services of a competent professional person should be sought.

Library of Congress Cataloging-in-Publication Data

Frigon, Normand L.
    The leader : developing the skills & personal qualities you need
to lead effectively / Normand L. Frigon, Sr. & Harry K. Jackson, Jr.
        p.   cm.
    Includes bibliographical references and index.
    ISBN 0-8144-7924-3
    1. Leadership.   2. Executive ability.   I. Jackson, Harry K.
II. Title.
    HD57.7.F7524   1996
    658.4'092—dc20   96-18401
                                                                      CIP

Printing number

10   9   8   7   6   5   4

Contents

Preface: Never Grab a Bull by the Tail

You can become a leader and influence others in business, civic life, government, and in your personal affairs. Leadership is active; there is no such thing as a passive leader. Therefore, you must constantly challenge yourself, challenge systems, and challenge others to act. As you face these challenges, you must be able to lead, overcoming opposition to your leadership and the natural resistance that always meets any change. If you are going to win the contest for leadership and meet all the challenges this position poses, you must understand leadership philosophy: careful preparation and using a structured approach. This philosophy encompasses leadership principles, traits, and skills, all presented in this book.

This structured philosophy of leadership provides a leadership model that everyone can implement successfully. You may be tempted to step into a leadership position without this guide, but in that case you will not understand the basic requirements of achieving and maintaining a leadership position. That is like trying to stop a bull by grabbing the most obvious handle, the tail. *Never* grab a bull by the tail. You will never stop the bull that way, and you cannot lead the bull from that position. The situation could get messy. Worse, you could get kicked by the bull, an experience you would never forget and one that could permanently damage your chances of becoming a successful leader. Leaders never place themselves in a position to lose.

This book is about the reality of leadership, a subject that has long been shrouded in myth and legend. The "natural-born leader" is a myth. Certainly there may be a small element of leadership that is intangible, but leadership is an art and science that you can learn. Once you understand these principles, traits, and skills and practice them, you will be able to implement them successfully.

A well-structured leadership philosophy will allow you to set up a winning situation, to be sure that *you* lead the way. *You* choose the place; *you* choose the time; *you* choose the subject; and *you* choose the encounter. That way you are always prepared to lead the bull, whether the bull follows you because you have its dinner or because you have a firm grip on the nose ring. A leader is a person who has the ability to get others to do *willingly* what the leader desires to be done. All leaders have a clear vision, shared by their followers, that is built from their underlying values and competence.

Successful leaders share a number of characteristics. They are:

- ▲ Effective communicators
- ▲ Guided by a vision that is shared by others who are willing to follow them
- ▲ Supported by an effective leadership team
- ▲ Effective champions of their cause
- ▲ Accomplished public speakers
- ▲ Effective managers
- ▲ Skillful planners

So what does it take to be a leader? The answer is that first and foremost it takes *desire.* Then it takes the ability to apply the principles, traits, and skills described in this book.

N.L.F.
H.K.J.

1

What It Takes to Be a Leader

A leader motivates others to action. Thus, it is the motivation of others and their actions that defines a successful leader. In other words, leadership is the art and science of getting others to perform and achieve a vision. Therefore, leadership is not only reflected in performance, no matter how good that performance is, but in accomplishment. The motivation and actions of your followers is an important measure of your leadership, but the only measure of your success is in achieving your leadership vision.

As a leader, your focus is on accomplishing that leadership vision, whether in a personal, community or charitable, business, political, or industrial forum. All of these environments share a set of basic principles, traits, and skills that work in concert with your personal values to achieve successful leadership. The question for you to answer is this: Knowing what is required to become a leader, do you have the desire?

Here we identify the basic requirements for leadership, pinpoint why they are important to your leadership, examine how you can assess your leadership capabilities, and help you determine what you need to accomplish to become a leader. Then you can concentrate on achieving your vision.

The Building Blocks of Leadership

Everybody wants leaders who are competent, honest, forward looking, inspiring, and successful. Those leaders as well know

1

how to create an atmosphere of trust. They genuinely care about their own contributions as a member of the team and as individuals. Followers build a bond with their leaders based on honesty and trust, so it is essential that leaders are always honest with their followers. They are forthright about bad news as well as good news. But it is also true that they do not have to tell followers everything, as long as they demonstrate that they care about the followers and have established a trusting bond. Demonstrated integrity has a great meaning and builds the trust bond needed to achieve a leadership vision.

Leaders focus on the future, and move in a progressive direction. The leadership vision is a view of the future shared with followers.

You may be a single individual leading or have a leadership team to assist in leading a large effort. No matter what your environment is, you can become a competent, respected, and successful leader by understanding the basic principles, traits, and skills and utilizing them as the underlying building blocks of your leadership vision (see Exhibit 1-1). You also need to comprehend how these three leadership elements mesh with your personal values, as displayed in the following list:

Exhibit 1-1. The general building blocks of leadership.

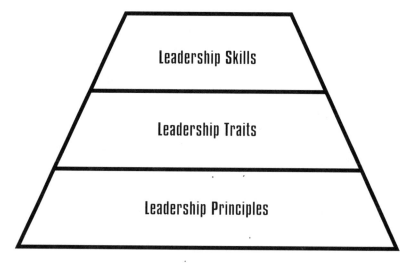

Principles	Traits	Skills
Integrity	Controlled emotions	Planning
Effective communication	Adaptability	Team leadership
	Initiative	Fiscal responsibility
Responsibility, accountability, and authority	Courage	Decision making
	Determination and resolution	Situational assessment
Positive mental attitude	Ethical behavior	Communication
	Sound judgment	Management
Consideration and respect	Endurance	Coaching
	Desire	Teaching
Constancy of purpose	Dependability	Facilitating
Teamwork		Effective meeting management
Effective resources management		Fact-based decision making
Fact-based decision making		Business knowledge
		Technical knowledge

Leaders achieve their vision by challenging, encouraging, enabling, coaching, and being a model for their leadership team and followers. Leadership is always a personal relationship between the leader and his or her leadership team and followers.

It takes still more to be a successful leader. As well as the basic principles, traits, and skills of leadership, a leader needs the specific skills of his or her vocation. To our knowledge, there are no generic leaders. All leaders are leaders of some specific enterprise. Civic leaders, musical leaders, political leaders, charitable leaders, business and industrial leaders, boy scout leaders, and all the others have one thing in common: the specific professional, educational, and organization skills and experience needed in their chosen field, as illustrated in Exhibit 1-2. These specific skills rest on the foundation of basic skills.

Among all these principles, traits, and skills, one trait is indispensable: desire. Without desire you will never become a

Exhibit 1-2. The specific building blocks of leadership.

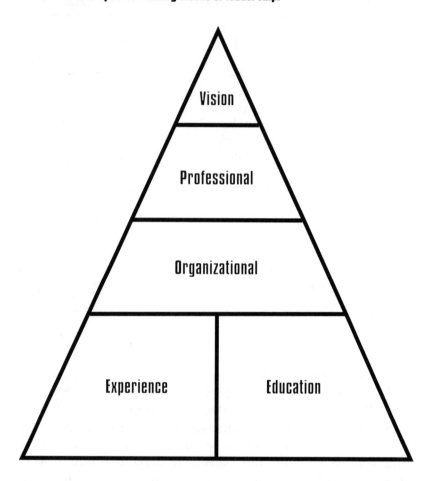

leader. You must have the desire to prepare yourself, to do what needs to be done, and to make the changes that need to be made. You must feel and demonstrate a passion for what you are doing, or you will never lead.

> *If there was ever a time in history when leadership was needed, it is now—not only the leadership of a few in high public office or the elite of the business community but leadership at every level of society, in every vocation and in every place. This need for leadership is the challenge that is your opportunity to lead.*

Leadership is an active process that requires a pioneering spirit and a willingness to take risks and be innovative. All good leaders are learners; they are students of past mistakes who benefit from all that has gone before rather than autocrats who seek to fix blame.

Workers will not follow a leader without a common vision that is inspirational. The leader inspires a shared vision that their followers accept. Inspired leadership is a passion that can ignite an organization to extraordinary accomplishments. Managers all too often are naysayers—the source of the final no that dampens innovation and slows progress. Leaders, in contrast, challenge the process and the system. They facilitate others to act and in the process instill a sense of teamwork that will go far beyond the individual relationship of the followers and the leader.

Leaders understand the building blocks of leadership and earn trust, respect, and loyalty by their actions and words. If you are not the model that they are looking for, all the authority in the corporate world cannot make you a successful leader. People do not undertake a job, profession, or skill without a desire to succeed. All employees potentially are good, successful workers; leadership is the key to unlocking that potential.

The Leadership Culture

A leadership culture is the pattern of activities that has been used to influence people, establish goals, perform planning, and make decisions. It determines the way people perceive and feel about their organization, its infrastructure, and its leadership. The leadership culture is the formal and informal way work gets done. Inherent in this definition is its tangibility. You can literally touch, feel, taste, hear, and read about the leadership culture, and you can certainly measure it by its results.

Despite the extraordinary changes in modern business practices and principles, our leadership culture too often remains closely associated with the classic autocratic approach to management. Whenever achieving a vision, goal, or objective becomes difficult, it is easy to abandon the basic leadership principles, traits, and skills and become an autocratic manager. This dinosaur makes decisions without consultation, then gives orders and expects immediate obedience. Since the autocrat does not seek the opinion of subordinates, creativity and innovation are squelched.

The traditional leadership culture requires close supervision and motivates through negative reinforcement. In this environment, the basis for legitimate leadership is formal authority. This system is task oriented and places little value on the development of good working relationships with subordinates. The workforce has reacted to this form of leadership by doing only what is compulsory and attempting to suppress its frustrations. Often we have seen these frustrations play out in aggressive behavior, verbal abuse, work stoppage, and sometimes sabotage.

In today's changing world, the pure autocrat has become an increasingly ineffective leader. As a successful leader, you should be prepared to challenge an autocratic culture and to act as a change agent. To do so, you must be able to assess your organization's culture or environment and establish a baseline of where you are now. You probably have an opinion about the culture, but this opinion may not be based on fact. The most effective method to assess culture is to conduct a survey—verbal or written, formal or informal. Typically it contains some of the following questions:

- What is your leadership path?
- What must you accomplish to succeed?
- What is expected of you?
- What are the taboos?
- What are the rivalries?
- Who holds the power?
- How do you get ahead?
- How do you stay out of trouble?
- What does this culture really value?
- What skills are needed to win?

Your challenge is to be a principal cause of positive change in your environment, whereby the autocrat becomes a leader of people, and autocratic companies stand up as leaders of industry in the new global economy. There is nothing else more difficult to accomplish, less likely to succeed, and more hazardous to a career than to initiate change. *This ability to lead change is the most significant management skill needed today.* Leaders who develop the skill to facilitate change in an organization will be the guiding force for the future.

Change and reorganization are universally feared. Change upsets the established order, introduces risk, and disturbs the status quo. For this reason, change and reorganization are often deferred, to the detriment of the organization, which experiences a loss of effectiveness, quality, and throughput and increases in cost.

Leadership Principles, Traits, and Skills

One of the results of your self-assessment will be an understanding of the principles, traits, and skills you need to become a leader. The leadership *principles* are the fundamental doctrines or assumptions governing leadership. *Traits* are the distinguishing qualities of a leader; they form the characteristics that you demonstrate as a leader. The *skills* are the hard sciences of leadership. They are where leadership and management merge. The principles and traits are what followers expect of their leaders. The skills provide you with the tools to win a leadership position.

Knowing, understanding, and implementing the principles and traits of leadership is half the model. Learning the skills is the other half. It is your implementation of leadership skills that will sustain you as a leader.

Remember one important point: Leadership is in the eye of the follower. You cannot declare yourself a leader and thereby make it so, regardless of your position. Leaders fulfill the expectations of their followers. The way to do that is to know, understand, and implement the leadership principles, traits, and skills that are required to lead in your environment. A good assessment of what you must do to become a leader is therefore critical to winning and sustaining a leadership position. It is also important for you to assess these requirements based on your basic values. Are you willing to do what is necessary to be a leader?

The Leadership Model

Leaders today are no longer defined by business, political, or social position or power. Rather, they are defined by their ability to perform and achieve their vision. The measure of a successful leader has become not what position he or she has achieved but what that person is doing in that position.

Realization of your vision as a leader occurs not through happenstance but by following a clear path. That path is the leadership model, shown in Exhibit 1-3, which builds on the basic leadership principles, traits, and skills you have acquired through education, training, and experience. These and your values are the basis for defining your leadership vision. Once you have identified your vision, you must do a leadership self-assessment to determine what you need to do to achieve that vision. Perhaps this self-assessment indicates a need for more training, or more education, or new skills. All this preparation and self-assessment will lay the groundwork needed to achieve your leadership vision.

This model is not intended to imply that the leadership process is linear. Change is one of the few constants we can be sure of, so you will be reassessing your leadership vision continually and updating the basic skills you will need to remain a leader.

Exhibit 1-3. The leadership model.

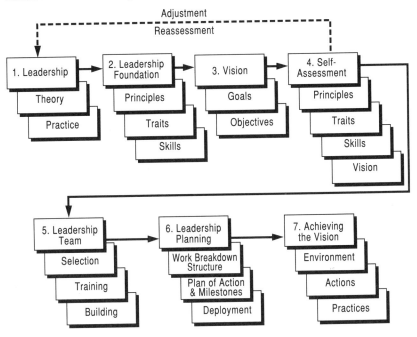

The first step in the leadership model is for you to understand the theory of leadership and how leadership practices relate to that theory. This is basically your initial decision point when you ask for the first time, "Do I have the desire to be a leader?" In the second step of the model, you must consider how you will lay the foundation for your leadership vision. Examine the leadership principles, traits, and skills and determine how these skills relate to your education level, knowledge, and values. After establishing your leadership vision (in the third step) and the goals and objectives needed to achieve that vision, perform the self-assessment in Appendix A to determine your status as a leader. This assessment (step 4) will answer the following questions:

- ▲ Do your personal values support the leadership principles?
- ▲ Do your value system and character provide for effecting the leadership traits?

▲ Do you have the skills, education, and experience to achieve and maintain your vision?

This self-assessment is designed to provide you with an understanding of where you are at today and what you need to do to become an effective leader. The assessment is divided into specific areas, as denoted by the following questions:

▲ What is your leadership profile for principles?
▲ What is your leadership profile for traits?
▲ What is your leadership profile for skills?
▲ What is your leadership profile for vision?
▲ What is your leadership profile for planning?
▲ What is your leadership profile for teaming?
▲ What is your leadership profile for communicating?
▲ What is your leadership profile for achieving?

Based upon this assessment, you may need to reevaluate and perhaps adjust your leadership vision or consider changes that may need to be made in your personal values, education, or training.

Step 5 in your process is to select your leadership team. Whom will you invite to help you achieve your leadership goal? The selection of your leadership team is based on the needed skills to achieve your leadership vision.

Next comes step 6, the management part of the leadership model—planning. You must understand the specific functions for achieving your leadership model, break those down into a work breakdown structure (WBS), and then formulate a milestone chart that visually presents the schedule for the WBS. These tools will assess your resource needs for achieving your leadership vision. From this point you can formulate your plan of action and milestones and deploy it to your leadership team and other followers.

Now you are ready to achieve your leadership vision (step 7).

The Essentials of Leadership

It is clear what we want from our leaders: honesty, competence, credibility, and a vision that we can share. If you are to lead, you must be able to communicate with confidence this winning image of the future. Then others can believe that you have the ability to take them there.

The leadership practice of inspiring followers with a common vision involves not only clearly establishing that vision in the mind of the followers but implementing it within a structure of principles, traits, and skills. This becomes a clear example of leadership that others are willing to follow. Living out your values is a practical way of demonstrating your honesty and commitment. We trust leaders whose deeds and words match. Trust is also a key principle of enabling others to act. Leaders trust their leadership team and others so that others will trust them.

Competence and business and technical knowledge are more concrete principles that a leader can demonstrate directly. Competence is determined by your demonstrated business and technical expertise. Succeeding at your craft is a sure sign that you have knowledge in that area.

When you follow this basic philosophy of leadership, you will attract others to what you represent. In a certain sense, you are managing your credibility. You are conscious of how your behavior affects others, and so you take charge of how others come to see you. You accomplish this with candor and principle, not by manipulation.

You can lead people through promises or coercion. Promise a bonus or threaten the loss of income, and you can get people to perform—in the short term. Autocratic managers and bureaucrats have proved this repeatedly in the past. However, when you understand the essence of leadership, everyone who works for you will be motivated by your vision. They will be there because they want to be, not because they have to be. Apply the leadership principles, traits, and skills to people; save your management skills for things.

> *Lead people. Manage things.*

There is a clear distinction between managing and leading. That distinction is between getting others to do and motivating others to want to do. Managers can get people to do things, but leaders motivate people to perform.

Putting It All Together in This Book

This book is organized around the basic building blocks of leadership. We begin with a discussion of the basic principles of leadership to provide you with a basic understanding of these principles, then proceed to learning the principles, implementing them, and applying them to your leadership. This same approach is used for the leadership traits and principles. Finally, we set out a leadership strategy that provides a blueprint for your leadership challenge and give you an understanding of how to become a world-class leader.

Chapter 2 begins building the foundation of your leadership by asking you to pose the question, "Do I have the desire?" This is the important first—and last—question in building the foundation of your leadership. You need to understand clearly that becoming a leader requires much more than simply wanting to. There is a significant difference between wanting to be a leader and having the desire and willingness to do what is necessary to achieve your vision. It is also the last question to ask yourself after you have read this book and understand exactly what you are undertaking. This chapter lays out in detail the basic traits and principles needed to achieve any leadership vision. The traits and principles are presented as everything else in this book will be presented: a discussion of *what* the trait and principle is, *why* it is critical to leadership, and *how* you can have and demonstrate this to your leadership team and followers.

Once you have a basic understanding of desire, principles, and traits, the next step is to understand how these mesh with your personal values and the values of your leadership environment. Chapter 3 gives you the leadership tools to know and understand your personal values and translate those values into a leadership vision. The chapter then goes on to explain how to establish goals and objectives needed to achieve that vision— all very real practical tools that you can use throughout your leadership career.

Always bear in mind that you don't do leadership alone; you need a strong leadership team. Chapter 4 thus explains the techniques of team building, team dynamics, and an understanding of the team phases and how to lead teams through these phases.

Management is a crucial part of leadership; you need to be capable of planning, estimating, controlling, and deploying your vision. Chapter 5 puts all this together using some of the most modern and up-to-date planning and management tools. It gives both new and seasoned leaders the skills to manage success.

All leaders at all levels in all environments meet resistance; knowing how to evaluate and overcome it is critical to achieving and maintaining your leadership position. Chapter 6 presents the 3Cs of leadership—communication, cooperation, and coordination—which are the best methods for gaining adherents and winning over those who resist your leadership. Other tools are needed too, and they are provided as well in Chapter 6.

All of the groundwork you have done in this book comes together in the final chapter, which prepares you to face the leadership challenge.

Appendices A and B contain the self-assessment and a leadership plan outline, respectively.

This book is designed to be a practical leadership manual that you can use for many years to come. It will form the basis for establishing you as a world-class leader and will serve as a model for you to select leaders in the future. The leadership book will not sit on your bookshelf; it will be in the center drawer of your desk.

2

Leadership Principles and Traits

The leadership traits and principles are the foundation upon which you will build your leadership. As noted in Chapter 1, the first question you must answer for yourself is, "Do I have the desire to become a leader?" In this first step you must know and understand who you are, where you want to go, who is going to come with you, and how you are going to get there. You need to be honest. Remember that you may be able to fool yourself, but others—your leadership team and those people who are your followers—will soon recognize if you have the desire, principles, and traits needed to be an effective leader.

A Question of Desire

Leadership begins with self-leadership. You must first focus on a specific goal and then develop the fire within to achieve it. Then, and only then, will you be able to begin to lead your team.

The goal of all human endeavor is to earn a profit and to build wealth. This is true for business, government, nonprofit organizations, and in our personal lives. This concept may seem unusual at first because we usually think of profit and wealth in terms of money. But in reality it encompasses a host of other resources, among them influence, customer loyalty, credibility, and increased demand.

A government agency or nonprofit organization, for example, earns a profit when it increases its efficiency and provides more services with the same resources (labor, material, equipment, and money). As this efficiency grows, there is an accumulation of wealth in terms of an ability to achieve more with the same or less, and increased customer satisfaction. In our personal lives, profit and wealth may be viewed in terms of savings, net worth, lifestyle, relationships, memories, experiences, and credibility. In business, the profit may be measured in other, more traditional terms, such as money or capital assets.

Leadership begins with you, first on a personal level and then spreading to those whom you would lead. Leadership is first a matter of understanding who you are and where you want to go. This is the focus we all need in our lives if we are to become fully actuated. Maintaining the focus to achieve our visions requires desire and persistence—a fire within. You must light this fire within, then motivate others so that their fire within is burning and you are all seeking the same vision. To light the fire within, you need to answer four questions:

1. Who am I?
2. Where do I want to go?
3. Whom do I need and want to go with me?
4. How do we get there?

Who Am I?

What do you stand for, and what are your skills and knowledge? You need this knowledge to select the visions that are appropriate for you to pursue in your life, your organization, or your team. It enables you to understand if you can accomplish the tasks assigned to you or the vision you choose for yourself. The answer to this question is important no matter how large or small the goal you seek to accomplish.

Understanding who you are requires that you understand your values and your competencies and limitations. Your values, the things that you determine to be of worth (perhaps honesty, love, security, money in the bank, status, recognition, fame), drive your choices and actions. When your actions are consistent with your values, the values become unifying principles, providing focus for your life. Your values therefore provide a focused approach to setting and achieving goals. When your actions are inconsistent with your values, this mismatch leads to stress, lack of constancy of purpose, lack of confidence, and chaos.

As a leader, it is important to understand the values of those you lead as well. If you ask them to perform tasks or work toward visions that are inconsistent with their values, they will quickly become dissatisfied and demoralized.

Understanding who you are also means honestly assessing your talents, knowledge, and experience—your competency. This insight, essential for success in all aspects of your life, enables you to understand:

- Your vision of what you want to achieve
- The skills and knowledge you need to develop for achieving your vision
- The skills and knowledge your team members need to complement those you possess

Where Do I Want to Go?

Deciding where you want to go is the vision you will focus on—the destination for your actions. This may be your personal vision, the vision handed to you by others, or the vision developed by your leadership team. Maintaining a focused vision provides the constancy of purpose required for success.

Vision encompasses what you want to accomplish in broad, high-level terms and also what *specifically* you want to accomplish—that is, your goals. The actions for achieving the goals are the objectives; they define how the goals are to be achieved. In the planning phase, you will identify the objectives until you have specific actions to be accomplished.

As you develop the objectives, you will see that they are goals at the next level of detail. Remember that goals are *what* we want to accomplish and objectives are *how* we accomplish the goals. This definition will enable you to take a long-term vision through medium-range goals, short-range goals, and then day-to-day activities.

Your vision may be a short-term assignment handed to you, a lofty vision for your entire organization, or what you want to accomplish with your life. It begins with the vision you want to achieve for yourself. Even when you are given an assignment, you will need a vision of what *you* want to achieve for yourself while accomplishing your responsibilities.

Whom Do I Need and Want to Go With Me?

Selecting your leadership team is a very important step, done *after* you have decided where you want to go. Selecting your team before deciding who you are or where you want to go is a fatal mistake, in both personal and professional life. In your personal life, it may result in potential not reached, dreams not fulfilled, and the destruction of relationships. Professionally, it may result in missions not accomplished, visions not achieved, personal and professional potential not reached, and the destruction of partnerships and businesses.

To select the individual or team to work with you in attaining your vision, you must understand the competencies required to assist you. These competencies may be technical or nontechnical; they may be complementary, redundant, or unique. Eventually you will need to expand this selection so that your entire organization comprises individuals with complementary and supportive competencies to achieve your vision.

How Do I Get There?

Developing and executing the plan to achieve your vision is a critical step that many fail to follow through on. With the appropriate planning and resources management, you will ensure your success.

In this step, you identify the action needed to achieve the vision (i.e., your goals and objectives), determine when each action needs to be accomplished and what resources are needed, select those responsible for completing each task, and determine the responsibility and accountability for each team member. Documenting this plan in a plan of action and milestone chart will enable you to ensure effective planning, track progress, and manage your resources.

Answer each of these four questions as thoroughly as possible *and in sequence.* If you answer them out of sequence, you will not have the focus necessary to achieve your vision. You may select individuals to assist you in attaining your vision who are incapable or unwilling to work toward your goals, or you may even select visions or goals that are incompatible with your own values or competencies. You will have constancy of purpose only if you answer the questions completely and in sequence.

This approach applies to your self-leadership and your leadership in all aspects of your life. It is the beginning that is needed to establish your purpose, maintain constancy of purpose, and provide the motivation to get others to perform.

Leadership Principles

The leadership principles are the comprehensive and fundamental concepts that are the foundation necessary for becoming a leader. You will need to practice these principles in all aspects of your life, personal and professional. You will begin by developing self-discipline and self-leadership. You are, after all, a leader to yourself and therefore need to possess personal or self-leadership.

Just as individuals seek to lead, organizations also seek to be leaders in their peer group (e.g., industry, social group, or athletic group). The leadership principles therefore need to be a part of the culture of the organization or team that you participate in or lead. There are nine leadership principles:

1. Integrity
2. Effective communication
3. Responsibility, accountability, and authority
4. Positive mental attitude
5. Consideration and respect
6. Constancy of purpose
7. Teamwork

8. Effective resources management
9. Fact-based decision making

Integrity

Integrity is the adherence to a high standard of honesty and character. It is a set of established values, with your actions consistent with these values. Character is what you are; reputation is what others think you are. When the values, character, and actions you present to others are consistent with your personal beliefs, that's integrity.

The most important leadership principle that you will demonstrate to your leadership team and your followers is integrity. From the perception of integrity will flow the consistency of purpose and the character that will motivate your leadership team and bind your followers to your vision, goals, and objectives. The most important component of integrity is the quality of personal character.

When you act consistently with your values, others will notice, and your reputation for living with integrity will develop. Those you choose to lead will notice and know they can count on you to act decisively according to your convictions. Integrity requires action.

> Integrity is not passive. *Integrity requires more than not doing anything that is contrary to your stated values. You must be active and consistently act on your beliefs and values.*

Acting in accordance with your values is living with honesty. This means avoiding deceptive communication, either overtly or by omission, and being open and frank about your values. Your values will be evident in the decisions you make and the actions you take. If your decisions or actions are inconsistent with your stated set of values, you will quickly earn a reputation as a fraud. Living with rigorous honesty will do the following:

- ▲ Establish a basis for confidence in your leadership for yourself and others.
- ▲ Build your self-reliance and self-respect.
- ▲ Establish a clear understanding of your motives and desires for yourself and others.
- ▲ Protect you from destructive controversies.
- ▲ Inspire you to progress toward your vision with great initiative.

A facade of integrity will never work. Pretending to have and abide by a set of values that are not truly yours and putting on a character that is alien to your true beliefs is difficult, stressful, and always counterproductive. Eventually your facade will crack, revealing your true values and character. If your true character is different from the face you have presented, your leadership team will lose confidence and trust, and your followers will lose heart and belief in your vision.

Consistency of purpose will establish a basis for confidence in your leadership for yourself, your leadership team, and your followers. Acting in accordance with your true beliefs and values allows you to be free and open. By answering the question "Who am I?" clearly and honestly, you know yourself—your values, character, and skills. This understanding builds your self-reliance and self-respect to make you the leader you want to be.

Being an integrity-bound leader will establish a clear understanding of your motives and desires for yourself and others. It will protect you from destructive controversies that always arise when the integrity of your actions is called into question.

Organizations are made up of individuals. Just as it is important for individuals to live with integrity, so must organizations. A group that acts without integrity will not have loyal members.

Effective Communication

Effective communication is clear, concise, and comprehensible communication through any medium. Leaders must be capable of communicating their values, vision, goals, and objectives in many different ways: in meetings and in personal, written, electronic, and organization communications.

> *All successful leaders are good communicators.*

Personal communication is the daily one-on-one communication that occurs with individuals on your team, with followers, or with others in your organization. This important form of communication is used in giving instructions, asking and answering questions, listening to concerns, and all the other daily communications that occur in any organization. You must make every personal communication a motivating one for your team and for your followers.

The written and electronic forms of communication include memorandums, formal reports, letters, meeting minutes, proposals, and e-mail. The leader must have the capability to convert his or her ideas into coherent written form. Although written communication is different from personal communication in its form, the focus is the same: an effective communication that results in understanding and action. Written communications can be just as easily misunderstood as any oral communication.

You probably spend significant amounts of time in meetings and must have the ability to conduct productive, effective, and efficient meetings. These meetings are a critical way in which you communicate with your leadership team and others, so be sure to avoid the pitfalls of a lack of focus, poorly defined purpose, no clear agenda, and no closure or follow-up.

Communication is your most important tool for carrying out all of your organization functions: planning, organizing, staffing and staff development, directing and leading, and evaluation and controlling. Poor communications is the most frequent cause of many organization problems, such as lack of management credibility and lack of trust. The resolution of these impediments could transform a failing enterprise into a successful one.

Communication is so important to leadership that we have devoted an entire section in Chapter 6 to this subject. In that chapter we will provide methods for improving communications.

Responsibility, Accountability, and Authority

Responsibility, accountability, and authority are inexorably tied to each other by definition and by function. A responsible leader must have the authority to act to be an effective leader, and everyone in a position of authority must be held accountable for his or her performance.

Responsibility is having the burden or obligation to accomplish something that is within your power to achieve. You and you alone have the responsibility for achieving your leadership vision. Your followers and your leadership team will hold you accountable for your actions and for your success, or failure, as a leader.

Accountability is the necessity to report on your actions, performance, or achievements. As a leader, you are, of course, accountable for your actions to your leadership team and to your followers, and you may be accountable to some higher authority. Accountability implies some obligation and even a personal (or business) liability for your actions. Just as you should and must hold others accountable for the authority you have delegated to them, you are accountable as a leader in a much broader way and to a much greater degree.

Authority is the power to act—both a legal right to act (such as the authority to raise funds, write checks, and submit documents) and often the right to act for the leader in his or her absence by signing letters and documents, issuing instructions, and managing resources. The authority to act and accomplish goals and objectives is a serious one. Everyone who has been delegated authority to act—the leader, the leadership team, and followers—must also be held accountable for the exercise of that authority.

> *You can and should delegate authority to your leadership team. Everyone in a position of authority and trust must be held accountable, but responsibility always rests with the leader.*

The success of many of your leadership activities depends on appropriate responsibility, accountability, and authority—both given and accepted. This applies in your personal, social, and professional life. You need to seek responsibility and be accountable for your actions. In performing your responsibilities, you must also have the authority to act. Often this authority is given with the assignment, position, or mission. If it is not, you need to take action to ensure that you have necessary authority.

Each individual needs to know what is expected, to understand that he or she has the authority necessary to accomplish a responsibility, and to realize he or she is accountable. Remember that what gets measured gets done.

Positive Mental Attitude

A positive mental attitude is the ability to focus on the positive aspects of your leadership and accomplishing your leadership vision, goals, and objectives. This attitude does not disregard the negative aspects that need to be considered but does not dwell on them. You are always looking forward and have a solution to every problem; failure is not an option. As a leader with a positive mental attitude, you would never say, "Oh my. We are short of funds for the project again. What will we ever do?" Rather you would say, "The project requires additional funding for successful completion. This is what we are going to do."

> Failure is not an option. *Decisions are made with positive direction for your leadership team and followers.*

Understand that you cannot control people, places, or things; you can only influence them by controlling your own behavior and attitudes. You can also influence the environment around you and the people you come in contact with each day. To influence others and to motivate them to achieve the things that you believe need to be done is your challenge. A positive mental attitude is vital to instilling this winning attitude in your leadership team and your followers.

We have all been exposed to managers and leaders who constantly emphasize the negative aspects of every situation. They are always gloomy and always disappointed. The influence they have is a negative one.

Your positive mental attitude will be reflected in your energy level. You will feel charged, and others will see you as someone with high energy and with a capacity for accomplishment, an important attribute for attracting loyal followers.

As you lead yourself and others, adhere to the principle of a positive mental attitude. This does not mean ignoring mistakes, failures, or negative influences but, rather, recognizing an equivalent benefit in every negative event. It is clearing your mind of influences that do not support a positive mental attitude, determining what you want, maintaining focus, and working to achieve your goals with steady persistence.

Consideration and Respect

Consideration and respect means the thoughtful and sympathetic regard for others. It is a return of the loyalty that has been given to you as a leader. You understand the impact of your decisions on others and are considerate of the consequences. You respect the rights and privileges of people for who they are and what they can accomplish.

> Leadership requires difficult decisions. *Difficult decisions concerning individuals can be made in a very positive way when you show consideration and respect for your leadership team and followers.*

Leadership often requires that you make difficult decisions that affect the future of others—disciplinary action, job assignments, promotions, training, and the like. You need to be able to make these tough decisions and to act on them, while treating all people fairly and without prejudice. By developing a genuine concern for the welfare, morale, and professional development of the individuals you lead, you are respecting them as individuals.

Effective leaders recognize that they cannot achieve success unless they achieve success for those they lead. When an individual or an organization is perceived as not caring about the members of the team, disaster looms. There will not be the loyalty and enthusiasm for your vision that is necessary for achieving great goals and objectives.

Constancy of Purpose

Constancy of purpose is the steadfast adherence to a set of principles, vision, goals, and objectives. This is more than just leadership focus; it is how you achieve your goals and objectives on your way to achieving your vision. Not only must you be focused on achieving your vision; you must be consistent in the application of the principles you employ to achieve it.

> *The outward behavior and performance of individuals and organizations is the result of constancy of purpose.*

The effective daily behavior of individuals and organizations reflects constancy of purpose that will provide you, your leadership team, and followers with a known, unswerving direction for your organization activities and individual efforts and will keep a sharp focus on your leadership vision.

Develop a clear vision and a passion for its accomplishment; then develop the appropriate planning and infrastructure for ensuring all actions are collaborative and supportive for achieving what you as a leader knows needs to be done. This includes selecting the resources necessary for achieving the goals and objectives and managing their application to all of the required actions.

Teamwork

Teamwork is the contribution of individuals through collaboration to meet a common goal. This is a cooperative and coordinated effort on the part of a group acting together.

All important leadership accomplishments are the result of a team effort. Effective leaders recognize this important principle and develop groups of people focused on achieving a measurable benefit.

> *There is no identifiable vision, goal, or objective that teamwork cannot accomplish.*

The growing complexity of leadership, business, and civic problems requires the knowledge of a collective team to overcome. The Wright brothers alone designed and constructed the first flying machine. The design, development, and production of the Boeing 777 required the collaborative efforts of thousands of people—a massive effort that started with a leader and a leadership team.

Individuals are limited by time, talent, capability, and capacity to achieve complex goals. Teams can achieve what cannot be accomplished by individuals.

Sometimes people seem to lack an ability to work together to solve problems. Establishing teams to accomplish a mission promotes a sense of collaborative goals and creates a sense of ownership so the team feels empowered.

Selecting and building a leadership team is so critical to your success as a leader that we have devoted a complete chapter to the subject. Chapter 4 imparts the skill and knowledge you will need to select and build an effective team.

Effective Resources Management

Effective resources management starts with a clear understanding of the resources (time, people, facilities, and finances) needed to accomplish your vision and the actions you must take to distribute and control them effectively. The optimum use of the resources available to you is effective resources management.

> *Leadership failures are most frequently attributed to the lack of or the poor management of resources.*

Effective leaders are skilled in developing plans to achieve their goals, which includes the judicious application of the resources to execute the plan. A leader who fails never attributes that failure to a lack of vision, instead citing the lack of resources to complete the goals and objectives: "We ran out of time [or funds or people]"; "The proper technology was not in place"; "We failed to estimate correctly"; and so forth.

You must identify the resources necessary to achieving your leadership vision and practice good planning, management, and financial skills. Then you will need to track and report on your plans. These important skills are covered in detail in Chapter 5.

Fact-Based Decision Making

Fact-based decision making is the selection of options based on demonstrable fact—usually quantifiable data, such as marketing studies, financial analysis, and statistical analysis. Decisions may also be made with qualitative data, although these may be more subjective because they depend on someone's determination of good and bad. But qualitative decisions can be just as fact based as quantifiable decisions if the information is gathered and evaluated properly.

> *Leadership is a continuous selection of options. Each option you select as a leader must be based in fact.*

As a leader, almost every decision you make and every option you select will be challenged and scrutinized. The best way to avoid any controversy is to use a fact-based decision-making process that is clear and definable. Leadership requires the continuous selection among choices—that is, choices among goals, courses of action, or individuals in planning, problem solving, or analysis. The most effective leadership is founded on the principle of fact-based decision making.

Making fact-based decisions means collecting all available data, performing the appropriate analysis, and selecting the best option. From time to time your decision may be contrary to the results of the analysis—perfectly acceptable as long as you document the reasons for your decision and have the analysis for future reference. Chapter 5 examines some tools used to make fact-based decisions.

Leadership Traits

Leadership traits are the distinguishing characteristics and qualities that set you as a leader apart from others. These traits are the personal attributes that you consistently demonstrate in exercising your leadership and management responsibilities. The importance of these traits cannot be overemphasized; failing to demonstrate any of these traits clearly to your leadership team will demoralize them and cause them to lose respect and confidence in you as a leader. An individual who successfully applies the leadership principles must possess these ten traits:

1. Controlled emotions
2. Adaptability
3. Initiative
4. Courage
5. Determination and resolution
6. Ethical behavior
7. Sound judgment
8. Endurance

9. Dependability
10. Desire

Controlled Emotions

Emotions are the demonstrated states of joy, sorrow, fear, hate, rage, and so forth. We all feel these emotions. As a leader, you will be disappointed in some individuals, will be joyful for successes, and may feel anger toward people or events. Whatever you may feel is fine; however, you must carefully control the public display of emotion and make leadership decisions based on fact, not emotion.

> *Nothing will alienate your leadership team or followers more quickly or more permanently than a temper tantrum.*

No one wants to follow a leader they fear, and everyone fears a leader whose emotions are out of control. This does not mean you are emotionless; there are certainly appropriate displays of emotion—joy in success and sorrow in loss, for example. It is the *inappropriate* display of emotion—rage, anger, peevishness—that will discredit you as a leader.

It is important to control your emotions rather than let your emotions control you. This does not mean that you need to become cold and dispassionate. It does mean that you need a strong sense of self-discipline. Avoid sarcasm and personal comments. *Never* use profanity. Focus on principles and facts, not personalities. If there is corrective action to be taken, do so without any display of pleasure or displeasure.

Adaptability

Adaptability is the ability to adjust to different situations, conditions, and circumstances. As a leader, you must be adaptable in two different ways: in the way you address and approach different people and as you face changes in your business, civic, or professional environments. Your ability to adapt to changes in the environment may well define whether you are successful in achieving your ultimate leadership vision.

> *Adaptability is a defining trait for all leaders and one that differentiates a leader from a manager.*

Change is one of the constant facts of life today, and the inability to adapt to it leads to sure failure. The realities of leadership are that circumstances will continuously change. Being a change agent is always risky. There are numerous forces that you will be unable to control, and they divert you from your chosen path of action. Be sure to develop the skill of rolling with the punches: accepting the things you cannot change, learning from them, and adjusting to maintain your constancy of purpose. Remember that your goal is always your leadership vision.

Initiative

Initiative means to be ready and able to initiate action. World-class leaders are always aware of what needs to be done; they do not need someone else to point out what to do. When the facts justify a decision, a leader must initiate action. One epitaph often heard for failed leaders is, "He lost the initiative and someone else got to his vision first."

> Lead or follow? *The difference between people who exercise initiative and those who don't is the difference between leading and following.*

Individuals with the ability to see the path to a leadership vision and take the initiative to get there will be the leaders of tomorrow. Taking the initiative, with the associated risks, defines the difference between leaders and followers.

Taking the initiative is not a spur-of-the-moment reaction but is coupled with fact-based decision making, with full knowledge of the risks and rewards. Once you have sufficient facts, make the decision. Notice we said *sufficient* facts, not *all* the facts, because often the initiative is lost in endless fact finding and discussions. There is always risk in taking the initiative. If the only actions you ever take are risk free, then you are a manager or follower, not a leader. Allowing your leadership team to take the initiative is part of delegating authority and accountability.

Courage

Courage is the quality of mind and spirit that enables you to face difficulty, danger, and pain (physical or emotional) with firmness and determination. This physical and moral control of fear gives you control over yourself and enables you to act in a threatening environment. Understand that courage is not the absence of fear; rather, it is resolve and determination that overcomes fear.

> *Courage is not the absence of fear but rather the presence of resolve and determination.*

You will win the respect and commitment of others by standing up for what you believe in and making tough decisions despite ambiguity. Effective leaders act in the best interest of the team, the organization, and their vision in spite of external threats. They confront problems and take action based on what they believe is right.

You can develop the trait of courage by understanding all the consequences of making a decision and deciding to accept those consequences.

Determination and Resolution

The characteristic of being resolute means being firmly fixed on a purpose or goal by deliberate choice and will. Determination and resolve are the traits that will get you from where you are today to achieving your leadership vision. Both are tied to the trait of courage.

If you are determined and resolved to achieve your leadership vision, then you will have the courage to face all situations necessary to achieve that goal. Moreover, your displaying these traits will encourage your leadership team and followers to perform during difficult times. If they see you staying the course and seeing the goals and objectives through to the end, they will do the same. But if you waver and grow weak, you will soon find yourself alone. You will have lost your credibility.

> *Demonstrating determination and resolve will encourage your leadership team and followers during difficult times.*

Once you have made a fact-based decision, you must maintain a focused effort to see it through to implementation. Do not alter your position on an issue except in the light of new facts.

Ethical Behavior

Ethical behavior is the system of values and moral principles that guides your conduct as a leader. It thus requires that you determine your values and act consistently with them at all times. Your ethical behavior reflects a basic philosophy for dealing with values and conduct with respect to the rightness or wrongness of your actions and the goodness or badness of your motives and vision. Ethical behavior and integrity are bound together in the same continuum. They are part of a single whole—one a principle, the other a trait—working together for the inspirational leader.

Ethical behavior is essential for establishing and maintaining your credibility and the loyalty of those you would lead. The best leaders exemplify honesty and integrity. They are forthright and honest in their dealings with peers, subordinates, and superiors.

By its very nature, ethical behavior extends beyond the

workplace into your personal life. Leaders can become discredited and fail due to their lack of ethical behavior in their personal lives. That is why the honest assessment of your basic values and desire to become a leader are so critical to your success. If these self-assessments are not totally honest, you will never have the ability to behave ethically. To demonstrate ethical behavior you must clearly understand what is expected of you (principles and traits) and be willing to live in that way.

Sound Judgment

Sound judgment is the ability to make a decision or form an opinion that demonstrates good sense and discretion. This means more than simply being decisive; your decisions must be well founded and make sense. Sound judgments are based on facts, knowledge, and understanding. This means you must review and analyze all of the facts prior to making any decision.

> *All leaders are decisive. Effective leaders have the ability to make sound judgments as well.*

Effective leaders are decisive, and they possess the ability to reach sound decisions promptly and to communicate them powerfully, directly, and clearly. Demonstrating this kind of sound judgment will win the respect of the leadership team, followers, and even adversaries.

Endurance

Endurance is the power to sustain your efforts without impairment or yielding to fatigue and time. There is a physical and mental dimension to endurance. As a leader, you will be expected to be physically able to meet your obligations. You may have to work long hours, travel extensively, attend apparently endless meetings, and be readily available to your leadership team and followers. Mentally, you will be expected to function as alertly at 10 P.M. as you did at 7 A.M., and you must be capable of mentally storing many facts and understanding many functions.

Endurance requires personal courage as well. You must have the ability to withstand physical and mental strain to see a job through to completion.

> *You must be physically and mentally fit to be an effective leader.*

We have all heard, "He would have been a good leader but he just wasn't up to the job." This is a leadership failure of endurance. The demands of leadership are such that you can become ill if you lack the endurance to meet the physical demands, and if you are not mentally fit, the consequences may be equally severe: emotional breakdown. Your self-assessment here must be totally honest.

You will need to develop and maintain physical and mental stamina. Mental endurance is tied to physical endurance; if your body is fit and capable, your mind can also be. Regular physical exercise for conditioning, proper diet, and an adequate balance of work and play will enable you to handle crises with competence, thereby developing and maintaining your high self-esteem and confidence.

Dependability

Dependability is the ability to place trust in someone else's actions. As a leader you must be relied on to keep your word in large things and small. This is the quality of character and self-discipline that means others can rely on you. They can rely on your word, your acting with integrity, and your loyalty. They know what you stand for, and they know you will stand up for what you believe in. Keep your word. If you say that you will be at a meeting at 8 A.M., be there. If you are committed to meeting a deadline, meet it. If you make a promise, keep it. Dependability is essential if others will follow your leadership.

> *Dependability is basic to leadership. Leaders who cannot be depended on will not be leaders for long.*

Desire

Desire is a strong craving that impels you to the attainment or possession of something that is real and achievable. This desire can be worthy or unworthy, and the possession can be good or bad. The point is that as a leader, your desire to attain leadership must be worthy of the efforts you are about to invest in attaining the vision. You must understand all the traits and principles of leadership, possess all the skills that will be required, and have the desire to attain your leadership vision.

> *Leadership is personal. It is based on your desire to achieve your vision.*

Having a desire to meet your goal is the essential catalyst for achievement. Desire is the trait that differentiates you from all others. It will give you the fortitude to develop all the skills necessary to be an effective leader, compel you to demonstrate leadership traits, and hold you to your leadership principles when the going gets rough, as it certainly will. To desire is to have a fire within that can be extinguished only by achieving your leadership vision. This desire will ignite your leadership team and sustain them.

3

Vision and Values

We hear more and more each day about time management, improved efficiency, and going faster. There is satisfaction in being able to do more with less and to achieve our goals faster, but speed and efficiency are meaningless without direction. We need a map and a compass for our journey, whether it is a career choice, vacation trip, building a house, or a business venture. The compass is a vision, and the map is the plan for achieving the vision.

Every human activity begins with an idea and a hope to achieve a desired future vision. Vision is what you want to accomplish; it is the target that you set. In order to achieve it, you need to maintain focus on it, and the members of your team need to understand it and believe in the possibility of achieving it as well.

Without a clear vision, you will wander aimlessly through life in all of your roles: parent, child, spouse, partner, employee, employer, civic leader, hobbyist. The vision may be a career choice, vacation trip, fund raiser, new product, new company, organization, or individual performance goal. In many situations, you will be given a vision by the organization you are a part of. Perhaps all the members of the organization share it. Even in this case, *you* will have an individual vision of what you want to achieve within the context of the vision given to you. This is what you want to achieve personally while achieving the goal of the organization.

Success as a leader depends on a clear vision that you are passionate about. You need to know what you want to achieve, believe that you can achieve it, and have a fire in your belly to achieve it. Your challenge as a leader is to communicate your vision to your team and to pass on to them your enthusiasm and passion.

What if you change your mind because of changes in your personal situation, technological advances, changes in the marketplace, changes in the economic or political climate, or even changes in your personal preferences? The answer is, "Not much." These changes are merely course corrections if you are true to your values.

Leadership Vision and Values

Personal satisfaction and success as a leader depends on your ability to achieve balance and harmony in your actions. This means understanding your values, developing a vision consistent with them, planning effectively to achieve your vision, and practicing good leadership in implementing your plan.

Your values are the standards that you use to decide what is good, how you satisfy your responsibilities to yourself and others, and how you judge your behavior and your accomplishments. The values guide the selection of vision and the data you collect, determine the way you evaluate the data, and ultimately guide your decision making.

Every organization has a set of values too, so your vision needs to be founded on the values common to you and your team. These values may be contradictory or even repressed; for example, some may value individuality and teamwork, or competitiveness and collaborative goal setting. These contradictions need to be addressed and resolved within the context of your vision.

If attaining your vision requires action that is contrary to your values or the values of your team members, there will be dissatisfaction and demoralization. Conversely, if the team members agree with the values of the leader and if the vision is consistent with that set of values, then achieving the vision is possible. Once there is consensus by your team about the values, the vision can be developed and a plan of action devised and implemented to achieve it.

Sometimes individuals or organizations publicly espouse certain values—"People are our most valuable asset," for example, or "The customer is king"—but their actions contradict these stated values. When this happens, the stated values are not consistent with the true values of the individual leader or organization leadership. The result is a lack of constancy of purpose, lack of confidence, and an atmosphere of chaos, stress, and low morale. Maximum effectiveness in an individual leader or organization exists only when the individual leader's or organization's stated values are consistent with the personal values of the leadership.

An existing organization may have established values, either written down or understood by everyone. The actions of the leadership team show what its members really value. When their actions are consistent with the organization's stated values, these values serve as unifying principles for all organization policies and actions. This provides a focused approach for establishing and achieving your vision.

The leader's or organization's values form the foundation of the organization's culture. If any group in the organization demonstrates a set of values contradictory to those of any other group in the organization, the two groups will be working at odds even though they may have the same goals. The values of the individual leader or organization provide a scale by which all behavior is ultimately judged. Groups with different values will therefore not have the same perspective in any given situation.

Shared values foster strong feelings of personal effectiveness among the members of the organization. They promote high levels of loyalty, develop consensus about goals, and instill a strong sense of ownership and caring about the individual leader or organization. These shared values are the foundation for focusing the organization to achieve a vision. Hence, the vitality of the organization depends on and is directly proportional to the existence of a set of values shared by all. It is imperative that every member of the organization know and subscribe to the organization values.

Establishing Your Values

One of your first tasks as a leader is to determine your values. You will need to compare them with the leadership principles, evaluate your performance for consistency with your values, and adjust your behavior as required. And when you select your team, you will need to ensure that there is consensus about the values and that the team's values are consistent with the organization's.

Establishing your personal values is a 6-step process:

1. Identify what you value.
2. Define your values.
3. Evaluate your values for consistency, synergy, and support of the leadership principles.
4. Evaluate your performance with regard to your values.
5. Adjust your performance to be consistent with your values.
6. Perform regular, periodic reviews of your values and improve as needed.

Step 1: Identify What You Value. This can be a painful experience if you haven't done it before. People often go through life reacting to their environment without consciously thinking about what is important. If you have reacted instead of responding in accordance with your values, you may be surprised to find that your actions have not always been consistent with what you value. Reacting is often a source of stress that is based on the inconsistency of actions and values as you consciously or subconsciously judge your behavior or accomplishments. Do not despair. You can change your actions in order to be consistent with your values.

You can use an affinity diagram to identify what you value. An affinity diagram is a tool for gathering language data in such diverse areas as ideas, opinions, issues, perceptions, or problems and organizing them into groupings based on the relationship between each. The steps that follow show how to go about it:

1. List everything that you think is important in your life. Write each item on a single sticky slip of paper (Exhibit 3-1a). Do not evaluate your ideas at this point.
2. Arrange the notes on a flat surface (a wall, a whiteboard, a window), grouping related ideas (Exhibit 3-1b).
3. Decide on a label for each group of ideas, with each label being an action statement. You may have to compromise among the ideas in order to include all of the ideas in a particular grouping (Exhibit 3-1c).
4. Review each item to see if it fits the category or should be moved, and review the labels as well to ascertain if any of the groupings can be consolidated.

The resulting affinity diagram brings order to a collection of apparently unrelated ideas. The labels are the values that you currently have. These may not be all the values that you need to be a leader, and they may not be consistent with who you want to be.

Step 2: Define Your Values. To understand your values, write a short paragraph about each of the values identified in the affinity diagram. This is a very important step because it solidifies what you mean by each value identified. Record this information. As you evaluate your values and compare them with vision statements, you will remember what your thought process was as you identified your values. Here are two examples:

1. Demonstrating the ability to interact refers to the ability to interact with people at all levels in a positive way. This is critical for leadership effectiveness because it will make everyone feel a part of your team, enhance communication and understanding, and foster harmony. To practice this value, you must first care about others, recognizing that they are important as individuals and that they have important contributions to make toward the success of the team and the achievement of your leadership vision. Then you need to treat all individuals with the respect that comes from this understanding.

2. Being efficient and effective as a leader means practicing time management and project management. Efficiency is the

(Text continues on page 45.)

Exhibit 3-1a. Preparing an affinity diagram.

a. Step 1: List what is important to you.

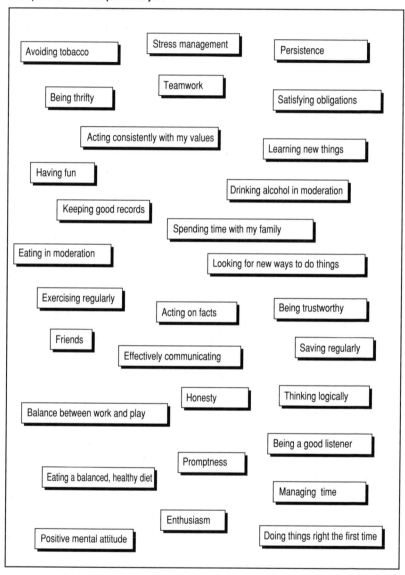

Avoiding tobacco

Stress management

Persistence

Teamwork

Being thrifty

Satisfying obligations

Acting consistently with my values

Learning new things

Having fun

Drinking alcohol in moderation

Keeping good records

Spending time with my family

Eating in moderation

Looking for new ways to do things

Exercising regularly

Acting on facts

Being trustworthy

Friends

Saving regularly

Effectively communicating

Honesty

Thinking logically

Balance between work and play

Being a good listener

Promptness

Eating a balanced, healthy diet

Managing time

Enthusiasm

Positive mental attitude

Doing things right the first time

Exhibit 3-1b.

b. Step 2: Group related ideas.

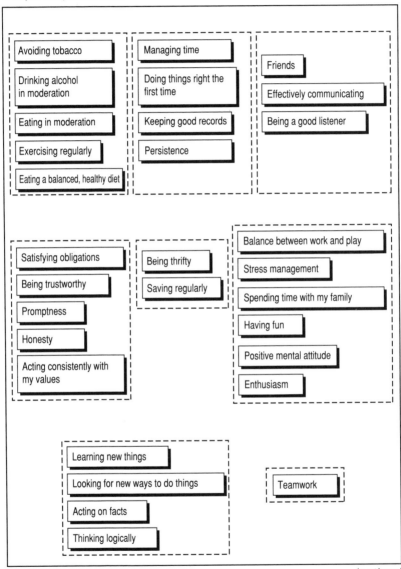

(continues)

Exhibit 3-1c.

c. Step 3: Assign labels to related ideas.

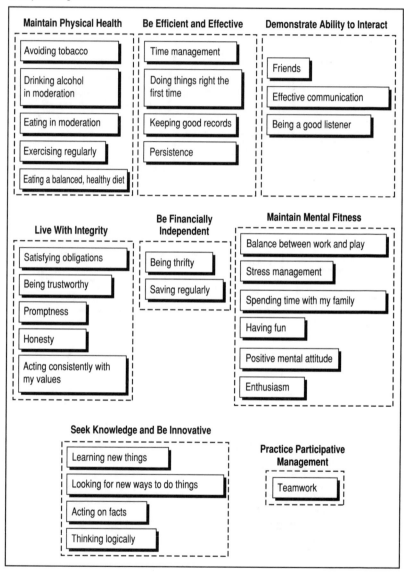

Maintain Physical Health

- Avoiding tobacco
- Drinking alcohol in moderation
- Eating in moderation
- Exercising regularly
- Eating a balanced, healthy diet

Be Efficient and Effective

- Time management
- Doing things right the first time
- Keeping good records
- Persistence

Demonstrate Ability to Interact

- Friends
- Effective communication
- Being a good listener

Live With Integrity

- Satisfying obligations
- Being trustworthy
- Promptness
- Honesty
- Acting consistently with my values

Be Financially Independent

- Being thrifty
- Saving regularly

Maintain Mental Fitness

- Balance between work and play
- Stress management
- Spending time with my family
- Having fun
- Positive mental attitude
- Enthusiasm

Seek Knowledge and Be Innovative

- Learning new things
- Looking for new ways to do things
- Acting on facts
- Thinking logically

Practice Participative Management

- Teamwork

proper and economical use of resources. To accomplish this, use the planning and project management tools. Effectiveness is prioritizing your efforts achieving your leadership vision. Therefore, efficiency means doing things well, and effectiveness means doing the right things.

Step 3: Evaluate Your Values. The next step is to evaluate your values for consistency, synergy, and support of the leadership principles identified in Chapter 2. You will do this with a relationship matrix that lists the leadership principles along the horizontal axis and your values along the vertical axis (Exhibit 3-2). Compare every item on the vertical axis with each item along the horizontal axis by asking whether the value supports the leadership principle. If the answer is no, leave the block empty. Otherwise, enter the corresponding symbol shown in the legend in the exhibit. When you finish, the pattern of symbols will be clearly evident.

Give each symbol the numeric weight indicated in the legend, and sum the columns and rows. The result will be a quantitative matrix that you can use to determine the adequacy of your values (Exhibit 3-3). The row totals reflect how well each leadership principle is supported by your values. Each principle needs to have at least one value that strongly supports it. The column totals show how each value supports all of the leadership principles. This information can be used to prioritize your actions— for example, in Exhibit 3-3, living with integrity has the greatest impact on practicing the leadership principles.

The column totals also tell a story. Living with integrity supports most of the leadership principles. The ability to interact has the next highest impact (overall). These two values are therefore the most critical for this individual. Being financially independent does not strongly support any of the leadership principles. It is, however, a value that is important for the individual in this example and cannot be ignored.

This evaluation is subjective in that it reflects the perceptions and opinions of the individual performing it. Careful definition and documentation of the values are critical for the evaluation because they provide some objectivity in that you understand the rationale for the evaluation and the decisions

(Text continues on page 48.)

Exhibit 3-2. Relationship matrix listing leadership principles and your values.

Legend: Strong = ⊙ = 9 Medium = ○ = 3 Weak = △ = 1 None = Blank = 0 **Values** → **Leadership Principles** ↓	A. Live With Integrity	B. Be Financially Independent	C. Be Efficient and Effective	D. Maintain Physical Health	E. Maintain Mental Fitness	F. Demonstrate Ability to Interact	G. Practice Participative Management	H. Seek Knowledge and Be Innovative	
1. Integrity									
2. Effective Communication									
3. Responsibility, Accountability, and Authority									
4. Positive Mental Attitude									
5. Consideration and Respect									
6. Constancy of Purpose									
7. Teamwork									
8. Effective Resources Managememt									
9. Fact-Based Decision Making									

Exhibit 3-3. Evaluation showing how your values support the leadership principles.

Leadership Principles ↓ / Values →	A. Live With Integrity	B. Be Financially Independent	C. Be Efficient and Effective	D. Maintain Physical Health	E. Maintain Mental Fitness	F. Demonstrate Ability to Interact	G. Practice Participative Management	H. Seek Knowledge and Be Innovative	Total
1. Integrity	●				●				18
2. Effective Communication	○					●	○		15
3. Responsibility, Accountability, and Authority	●	○	●						21
4. Positive Mental Attitude	●	△	△	●	●	○			32
5. Consideration and Respect						●	●		18
6. Constancy of Purpose	●		●				△		19
7. Teamwork						●	●		18
8. Effective Resources Managememt	△	○	●						13
9. Fact-Based Decision Making	△							●	10
Total	41	7	28	9	18	30	22	9	164

Legend:
Strong = ● = 9
Medium = ○ = 3
Weak = △ = 1
None = Blank = 0

that you make regarding it. You will need to review the matrix periodically to verify that it remains in sync with your values over time.

The result of this process is a powerful insight into the data you have developed. You can act on this information directly or use it to develop a plan of action. Remember that this process develops information from brainstormed issues or questions. The value of this analysis is in developing information. How you act on it depends on your knowledge, experience, or intuition.

It is important to realize that your values are what you think is important today and how you judge the world, your actions, and your accomplishments. These may change over time. This does not mean that there are no absolute goods. It does mean that in a given situation you may need to add a value that you haven't recognized as important in the past. It also means that as you periodically review your values, performance, and accomplishments, you will refine and improve the definition of the values.

Step 4: Evaluate Your Performance. Once you have determined, defined, and evaluated your set of values against the leadership principles, it is time to evaluate your performance, according to the following steps:

1. Make a list of your roles (parent, child, spouse, friend, employee, employer, civic leader, etc.).
2. List the goals you have for each role.
3. Review your actions, accomplishments, roles, and goals. Ask yourself if they are consistent with your values.
4. Describe why they are or are not consistent with your values.

Many leaders find that as they evaluate the requirements for achieving a vision, their values do not support that vision. You will be faced with similar situations in all your roles, and it is important that you recognize the importance of your values and understand the need to act consistently with them. If you act in a manner that is contrary to any of your values, this will set up a situation of turmoil and stress that will lead to failure. Sometimes you may be given an opportunity that is consistent with one of your values but not strongly supported by another value. There is a limit associated with each of your values that only you can determine. There are no easy answers or tools to assist in the evaluation. For example, if living with integrity and achieving financial independence are values I possess, I cannot accept an opportunity that provides great wealth but is illegal. I may choose, however, to abandon a lucrative career for a position that provides a subsistence-level income but a great deal of personal satisfaction. In the latter case the amount of the subsistence level that is acceptable may be different for two individuals with the same values.

Step 5: Adjust Your Performance to Be Consistent With Your Values. The assessment of your performance is the foundation for future action. When your actions, accomplishments, roles, and goals are not consistent with your values, decide on a course of action to change this situation, develop a plan and a timetable for implementing the actions, and then follow through.

Step 6: Perform Regular Reviews of Your Values. Plan to review your values at least quarterly. Go back to Step 1 and work through this process with the latest set of values.

Establishing Your Team's Values

You need to establish the values of your team just as you did for yourself. Each team member will have his or her own set of personal values. If they do not, have them use the six-step process.

To establish the values for your team, use the six-step process with all of your team members participating. The resulting set of values will guide the selection and definition of the team's vision and goals. These values are in fact how the team selects action and how it analyzes and judges actions and accomplishments.

The best situation is if all team members hold values that are consistent with your personal goals, and these are all consistent with the organization's values. This is rarely the situation. But as long as the sets of values are compatible, the team will be able to reach consensus about its values and the vision. If any values held by any of the team members are in conflict with your values, you will have to resolve that conflict. The methods for dealing with this situation are presented in Chapter 4.

If the organization's values have been defined and the behavior of the organization is consistent with the stated values, comparing your values and those of your team with them is easy. When there are inconsistencies with the behavior of the organization and the stated values or if the values have not been defined, use Steps 1 through 4 of the six-step process to identify the values of the organization. If your values are in conflict with the organization's, you will have a problem because this mismatch will result in turmoil and dissatisfaction for you as the leader. This is a prescription for failure. If you are unable to resolve this conflict, you will have to leave.

Developing Your Leadership Vision

Your leadership vision depends on the scope of your activities. Is this a personal vision, an organization vision, or the vision for an element of an organization or individual project? Once you have identified your vision, you need to communicate it to your followers and convince them that they have a stake in it.

The most effective method for developing a vision is with the participation of the leadership team. In fact, the very process of defining the vision in this way increases ownership among the team members and reduces the time and energy required to communicate the vision. It creates a body of visionaries and marketers for the vision.

Visions as Collaborative and Supportive

Team visions can be achieved only if the proper infrastructure is in place, and if your vision is synchronized and effectively deployed throughout the entire organization. In this way, the overall vision of your team is integrated with the vision of your part of the organization and your followers. The result of these actions is the integration of goals and objectives that support one another and ensure success in achieving the team's vision.

The development of a vision is a process. It has inputs, points where the input is processed, and outputs. It is a repetitive activity, in that the vision is constantly reviewed, clarified, revised, and improved. The leader and the team establish the vision and see that it is deployed systematically throughout the entire organization.

In the absence of top-down leadership, this technique for developing a vision can be used at any point in the organization. That is, an individual or a single organization element can develop its vision and deploy it throughout the organization that it controls or affects.

The Past as the Way to the Future

To develop the individual leader or organization vision, the team must project itself ahead in time and focus on possibilities. This challenge of developing an image of a possible and desirable future situation requires extensive effort and often takes a long time to accomplish.

One way to project the future is to examine what you know. What do your experiences tell you about the trends in your field, industry, technology, markets, customers, or resources? This study of the past is an essential element of the process of developing a vision, for the past is a prologue for the future. And just as the past is a resource of knowledge and experience, the present is an opportunity to apply these resources in developing the vision of the future.

Intuition plays an important role in developing a vision. Developing a vision requires that the logical, rational, and calculating (left) side of the brain assimilate data. The intuitive, creative, and verbally inarticulate side develops insight or makes decisions. The left side of the brain then arranges and puts into words the insights of decisions of the right half.

At work, however, many people act as if they were afraid that their peers would look down on them if they use their intuition for decision making. Intuition is sometimes viewed as a soft, mystical subject, and so we usually do not admit or discuss using it.

A vision or intuitive insight results from picturing and

imagining—the process of bringing together knowledge and experience to produce new insights. This knowledge, gained through an analysis of experience stems from an understanding of how and why things happen and who gets them done. The longer and more varied the experience is, the more likely it is that you will develop a deep understanding of a given set of facts or circumstances.

Intuiting is the conscious or subconscious act of drawing on past experiences to view a set of facts, perceptions, or circumstances. It includes selecting the relevant information, making appropriate comparisons, integrating the information, seeing patterns of change, and extrapolating from the present trends to future possibilities. This is right-brain thinking: scanning possibilities over space as opposed to time, thinking in images, seeing wholes, and detecting geometric patterns.

No Involvement Equals No Commitment

As a leader you can develop your vision by yourself but then will need to sell the team members on it. Your team must understand that they have a stake in achieving the vision, believe that the vision is important to achieve, and realize that it is possible to achieve. The team approach to developing a vision ensures commitment and ownership by the leadership team and also capitalizes on the experience, knowledge, and synergy of each member.

You can develop a vision independently at any level in an organization, company, or activity. In this situation, you work with what you know and what you are given. The resulting vision provides improved focus and direction and can be deployed throughout the parts of the organization you control or influence. This effort will advance you toward achieving your leadership vision but may be limited if there is a lack of continuity with individual leaders or organization executives and the other elements of the organization.

The Vision Development Process

The leadership vision is developed by a systematic process that ensures that the leadership team uses all available information and effectively analyzes it, leads the team to collect the required missing data, and provides a method for ensuring that the vision is consistent with the values of the leader, the team, and the organization.

This process of developing a vision begins with knowing and understanding your enterprise and all of the associated business, social, economic, and political environmental factors. Once the data are organized, evaluation using a brainstorming method provides the basis for drafting the individual leader or organization vision. This process has three steps: data collection, brainstorming, and creating the vision.

Step 1: Data Collection. As you reflect on the past and project to the future, the vision will not reveal itself perfectly formed. It needs to be carefully stated, periodically validated, and continuously refined and clarified. To achieve these results, the team members need to establish what they know and what the team and its sponsor or customers desire.

As data are collected, maintain a master file and ensure that each team member has the latest information. Each team member then reviews the data prior to each meeting and for completing his or her action items.

Begin the data collection by gathering the givens. For an existing organization, this is information about the enterprise that already exists. Some of it is understood, and some is formally defined. If any required items are not formalized, develop them from the facts you know about your organization as it operates now, and write them down. For a new organization this information is developed for the first time. All of this information will be verified, validated, and revised in the process of developing the vision.

Here are some of the items you will need to collect information on:

- Statements of values
- Mission statements
- Firm future business (such as orders and contracts)
- Plant facilities plans
- Manufacturing strategies and plans
- Current market survey

- Lists of customers (internal and external)
- Customer (internal and external) requirements and level of satisfaction
- Lists of organization and personnel expertise and specialties (core competencies)
- Employees' desires and expectations

The team must then review all of this information, discuss it, analyze it, and reach consensus about it. This understanding serves as the baseline for the next step: brainstorming the vital issues.

Step 2: Brainstorming. Brainstorming means free association. Each person presents his or her idea or response to a given item. The discussion is focused on clarification and drawing out additional ideas, not evaluating each point. Procedurally, each idea or response is written on a single sticky note. After you have exhausted the questions, usually after one hour, develop an affinity diagram as you did in establishing your values.

The issues you brainstorm will concern both the vital issues for your organization and more personal ones. The following questions are recommended to focus on the vital issues affecting your organization:

- What are the external forces that could affect our organization—for example, technology, market trends, and social or economic initiatives?
- What are the environmental issues that are likely to affect our organization in the near term and in the future—for example, laws, geography, demographics, climate, and national versus international issues?
- What are the economic and resource issues that will affect our organization in the future—for example, demographics, constituents, and the state of the economy, nationally and internationally?

A separate brainstorming session is needed to address the important questions concerning the personal desires and ambitions of the leadership team. It will develop an understanding of the personal desires of the team members and lead to consensus about the desired nature of the organization and its culture in the future. It will also help define the future roles and relationships of the members of the leadership team. Here are relevant questions to ask:

- What do we want the organization of the future to look like or act like?
- What future would we invent for the organization and ourselves?
- What is our personal agenda?
- What contributions would we like our organization to make to society?

Step 3: Creating the Vision. Now that you have a large amount of data about your enterprise—the givens, customer requirements, team members' desires and expectations, core competencies, and vital issues affecting the organization—you can analyze and reflect on this information and use it to start formulating the vision. Reach consensus about it, and then draft a statement of the vision, remembering that it is a statement of *what* you want to do, not *how* you are going to do it. Those details are developed in Chapter 5.

The length of the vision statement will vary, depending on the organization structure, nature of the business, and size of the individual leader or organization. It is not cast in stone; rather, it is a living document, continually held before the organization, continually tested, and continually modified to adapt to changes in the market and business information.

Effective Vision Statements That Challenge and Excite

The vision statement provides the direction for the team. It needs to be articulated in clear and exciting language. It is most effective if it is challenging but provides the latitude for flexibility and innovation in day-to-day operations. It is the basis for developing strategies and mission statements and for making decisions about conflicting courses of action.

An effective vision statement is unique. It differentiates the team or organization from others and tells those inside and outside the organization what is unique about it. This uniqueness fosters pride and boosts self-esteem and self-respect. Once the vision is established, it will be used to develop the plan of action and milestones for achieving it. This is a set of goals and actions with roles and responsibilities for achieving the vision. Here are some diverse examples of vision statements:

- ▲ We will be the supplier of choice for moving people and goods throughout the northeastern United States.
- ▲ I will become an internationally recognized expert in business improvement. This recognition will come from speaking, teaching, consulting, and being published.
- ▲ We will establish the leading institution of higher learning for the application of statistics to business and science.
- ▲ I will establish and lead a highly profitable enterprise, cost effectively, producing world-class quality products and services. We will focus on the design and production of manufacturing equipment. We will challenge the global marketplace, and do so while expressing a continual organizational commitment to social responsibility.
- ▲ We will establish and lead an organization of volunteers dedicated to supporting the needs of our high school athletic teams. Through the active support of parents, teachers, and students, we will raise funds through work projects and business sponsors to ensure that our athletes have the necessary equipment for the safe practice of their sports. We will establish the infrastructure and teamwork to accomplish this so that the maximum number of students are involved. And, we will have fun doing it.
- ▲ I will establish a business that will be the primary resource for business documentation improvement in the United States.

▲ I will become President of the United States. I will develop a leadership team that will capitalize on my successes in order to raise the necessary funds, establish an infrastructure capable of implementing a political campaign resulting in my party's nomination, and lead my party to victory.

4

Your Leadership Team

By nature the values and behavior we manifest are individualistic rather than collective. We have always prized individual visions, goals, and achievements. It comes as no surprise, then, that we admire the individualistic leader. It appears to us that all the memorable leaders of the past were strong individuals who overcame the odds and triumphed as individuals. That impression is wrong. Every leader in every environment, from Attila the Hun, to George Washington, Andrew Mellon, and Mother Teresa, needed the support of dedicated, loyal followers. They needed a leadership team.

Leadership today bears no resemblance to that of the past. The old command-and-control type of leadership cannot thrive in the technically complex, multifaceted, rapidly changing environment of organizations today. Modern organizations must keep current on evolving technology and markets, employ a workforce that is diverse in its makeup and location, and deal with communication that is instantaneous. No individual can cope with all the requirements of leading these many different activities alone.

All successful leaders have a committed leadership team. What makes the executive steering committee of a large corporation, a college football team, and the partners in a small business successful are the same basic characteristics:

- ▲ A clearly stated and shared vision
- ▲ Goals and objectives that are both challenging and achievable

- A team structure that is designed for success
- Competent team members
- Specific standards of performance
- Leadership that embodies the principles and traits of leadership
- A commitment to achieving

The new leader's role is to have the leadership vision, provide the resources, and create the culture to accomplish the goals and objectives that will achieve that vision. Future leaders are those individuals who understand how to work with teams that have the diverse skills, talents, and capabilities needed to lead modern organizations. Your leadership team is therefore a vital part of your becoming a successful leader.

It is a myth that leaders, like eagles, always fly alone. A successful leader is always first the leader of a team, and that team is a vital part of your work. You must have the competence to select, coach, facilitate, and lead your team. There are three elements to building your leadership team: team building, team dynamics, and team phases.

Team Building

In the movie *Patton,* George C. Scott, as General Patton, gives a poignant speech in which he states that the "individuality stuff written about the Army, in the *Saturday Evening Post,* is a bunch of crap. . . . An army is a team, it works as a team, eats as a team, sleeps as a team and fights as a team." This same statement can be made about all other leadership endeavors, both large and small. All important accomplishments are the result of a team effort.

Achieving your leadership vision is your challenge as a leader. As you identify goals and objectives, you will find that they cut across many functions and require specific skills, knowledge, and abilities, some of them outside your personal area of expertise. Moreover, you cannot do everything alone. You must get others to perform what needs to be accomplished. This means teamwork.

> *All great leaders of the past and present have one thing in common: a leadership team that is loyal, motivated, collaborative, and knowledgeable.*

Establishing your leadership team—a working group, a task force, a self-managing team, a council, a booster club, a partnership, and so forth—to accomplish a vision promotes a sense of collaborative goals. Furthermore, tasks that require people to exchange ideas and resources reinforce the notion that the participants share your collaborative vision. This teamwork creates a sense of ownership, and those involved will feel empowered. When people feel empowered, they are more likely to use their energies to produce the results you desire.

Effective leaders build teams and empower others to act. They involve others in planning and give them discretion to make decisions. They enlist the support and assistance of all those who must live with the results and make it possible for others to do good work.

As you select your leadership team, keep your vision in focus. The individuals on the team must have the requisite technical and business skills. Often they supplement your knowledge. If you are strong in design and development, you may need to seek team members who have strong financial, marketing, and production skills. If you are a business entrepreneur who excels at the organization and financial part of achieving the vision, look for members with strong technical skills on your team. Your team should provide the talent and expertise you are missing in yourself or your organization to achieve your vision.

Types of Leadership Teams

There are two basic types of leadership teams: functional and cross-functional. A *functional team* comprises individuals who do the same type of work to accomplish a specific goal. A functional leadership team therefore would be formed to accomplish some specific narrowly defined leadership goal, such as improved finances or better designs, marketing, or productivity. The members of a functional team have specific talents that contribute to the accomplishment of a functional task.

A cross-functional leadership team comprises individuals with different talents and competencies and is formed to accomplish broader tasks in accomplishing leadership vision, such as achieving strategic business improvements, establishing a small business, or winning an election. A cross-functional leadership team is better for achieving your leadership vision because it brings together all of the individuals necessary to understand the many diverse goals and objectives that your vision encompasses. Cross-functional teams require team members from across professional, technical, and organization boundaries.

Your particular vision, goals, and objectives determine whether you select a functional or cross-functional team. In either case, the team is a means to accomplishing your vision, not an end in itself. You will most likely have a cross-functional team as your leadership team but perhaps also several functional teams within your structure to address specific goals and objectives. These teams may be led by you directly or by the leadership team member responsible for that area.

If you are a senior executive, your cross-functional leadership team addresses overall issues of achieving your leadership vision, such as planning, policy, guidelines, finance, marketing, communication, and infrastructure. This team typically comprises the leader and your supporting team, which may be drawn from the leaders and managers of functional areas. In this case team members are also operating members of your organization.

A functional team is established to resolve a specific problem, improve a specific process, or achieve a specific goal or objective. Once it has accomplished its vision, it disbands. The solutions, products, services, or improvements it develops are maintained by the leadership team.

Work cells and self-managing work teams can be cross-functional teams of all the members of a particular process. They are responsible for completing a well-defined segment of a finished product or service. For our purposes, a work cell maintains the traditional hierarchical leadership structure. A self-managing work team, by contrast, is a group of employees that assumes a major role in such activities as planning, priority setting, organizing, coordinating, problem solving, scheduling, and assigning work. Regardless of the type of team, the team dynamics are the same.

Team Members

The success of your leadership team depends on selecting the right people who will accomplish your stated goals and objectives. They may be key people in your organization, the heads of departments or sections in large organizations, members of your department, influential people in civic organizations, or your partners in an entrepreneurial enterprise.

> *Qualified, enthusiastic leadership team members will contribute the most to achieving your leadership vision.*

Select team members carefully. They must be competent and capable of filling the need of the team, able to work well on a team, and loyal to you and leadership vision. Never choose them because of friendship or family relationship. If you say, for example, "Joe should be on the team because he is so interested in the topic," "I really can trust cousin Fred and his feelings may be hurt if I leave him out," or "Lillian has been here a long time and deserves a crack at this leadership team," your team will be doomed to failure.

Leadership team members typically have the following qualifications:

▲ They are *technically or professionally competent* in the skills you need. You can identify good candidates based on education, job experience, membership in professional organizations, qualifications such as CPA, or your personal knowledge of their qualifications.

▲ They are *effective communicators*. They are capable of communicating verbally and in writing with their peers, the other team members, and also with followers, other employees, the public, and maybe even the media.

▲ They *work well collaboratively*. Being a team member means being willing to discuss, brainstorm, listen, and accept consensus decision making. This is a trait that is just beyond some super egos. Someone who cannot work collaboratively with others can be disruptive to the leadership team and could prevent you from achieving your leadership vision.

▲ They are *personally responsible*. They have a reputation for getting the job done on time and controlling their emotions. People who have outbursts, pout when the decision does not go their way, perpetually miss deadlines, and come to meetings unprepared will disrupt team efforts.

▲ They are *available*. Often the individuals you desire on your team are busy people, so be sure they have the time and availability to focus on the leadership team efforts. Asking an eminently qualified person to be a member of your team is of little use if he or she never shows up at team meetings.

Your selection strategy must attempt to capture all of these qualities. Having team members who do not meet these basic standards will obstruct accomplishing the business of team and inhibit you from accomplishing the leadership vision.

Team Dynamics

Team dynamics are the phenomena that occur within teams as they operate. They affect the focus, motion, and equilibrium of the team. In the physical sciences, dynamics are the result of input, the environment, and predictable phased changes in the system. The input is the team structure, the roles of the team members, and how the team is trained and prepared. The environmental dynamic is the team's activities—they are chartered, organized, and executed.

> *Team dynamics resemble the physical sciences, there are specific team inputs, operating environments, and predictable outputs. As a leader you must control the first two to produce the predictable desired result.*

Team Structure

The structure of your leadership team is how the team is organized. Each member of the team has a specific role, vision, or goal as a member of the team. The team fits together in accomplishing those goals.

Experience with leadership teams has repeatedly demonstrated that a successful leadership team begins with a well-established structure, which encompasses your active support and a membership with clearly defined roles and responsibilities. Operating in a team environment may be a new experience for many team members, and we find that teams are more effective if they receive extra training in project management, team processes, management and planning tools, and fact-based decision making. In the successful leadership structure, each team member performs one of four roles: team leader, team members, facilitator, or adviser.

Team Leader. A leader has the capability to motivate others to perform what needs to be done. As the leadership team leader you have the sole responsibility for achieving your leadership goal. The authority, accountability, and responsibility for achieving your leadership vision is in your hands.

You are the team leader because it is your vision that you are going to achieve. As the leader it is your responsibility to manage and lead the team. You call and may facilitate meetings, handle and assign administrative tasks, orchestrate team activities, set team meeting agendas, and oversee preparation of reports and presentations. You must be directly involved in solving problems and must be reasonably good at working with both individuals and groups. If you want to achieve your leadership goal, you must lead this team effectively.

Effective team leaders share their authority with team members, whom they hold accountable for their performance and accomplishing goals and objectives. As the leadership team leader you are responsible for:

- Setting meeting times and agenda
- Conducting the meetings
- Resolving conflicts
- Solving problems
- Being a full-fledged team member
- Retaining your authority as the leader
- Being responsible for the records and minutes of all meetings

As the leader you are the central point of contact for team members. You are there to resolve any problems they may have and assist individual members. You must coordinate and set the times for the meetings and establish the agenda. Then you conduct the meetings, ensuring that they stay on track according to the agenda.

You should maintain the meeting minutes and assign any action items. With a small leadership team, you may do this yourself. In larger teams, you may have an administrative assistant or someone else to take notes. Whatever the size of the team, you should keep the minutes yourself to retain your perspective and focus. If another team member is the recorder, the perspective will be tainted by that person's responsibilities.

Your leadership team will operate effectively if you establish a good team structure and team activities. As the team leader, you must do the following:

- Be committed to achieving your leadership vision.
- Practice conflict resolution.
- Keep the team on track and focused.
- Be scrupulously fair and impartial.
- Be open to new ideas from team members.
- Do not compromise the team's goals or objectives with political issues.

Team Members. The team members, either individuals from the functional areas of an organization or people you have drawn together because of their individual talents, carry out assignments and accomplish goals and objectives. These individuals meet regularly with you and are essential if you are to achieve your leadership vision. Their number should be kept to the minimum necessary to accomplish the associated goals and objectives. There may be others, *ad hoc members,* who contribute to your success but do not meet regularly with you. These members possess specialized skills or knowledge that the team needs to address particular issues or actions.

Your team members must have a realistic understanding of their role in the leadership team and in achieving the vision. They must:

- Know and understand their roles as members of the leadership team.
- Have the skills and capability to make fact-based decisions.
- Be able to work as team members.
- Be in agreement with the vision of the team leader.
- Have the time and resources to be a team member.

Facilitator. The facilitator, a specialist trained in all the management and leadership tools, works with you and the team to keep everyone on track, provide training as needed, and facilitate the application of the appropriate tools. The facilitator must possess a broad range of skills in group process, effective meetings, conflict resolution, effective communications, total quality, and training. This person brings extensive knowledge of management and leadership tools and experience in conflict resolution.

The facilitator is not a member of the team and does not participate in team discussions or vote as a team member. The role of the facilitator is limited to:

- Keeping the meeting on track according to the agenda provided
- Providing management and leadership tools to help the team discussions

▲ Resolving team conflicts that arise during meetings
▲ Providing training to the team

Frequently the facilitator is a consultant who is hired specifically to facilitate meetings. As the team begins performing and the tools and skills become known to team members, the facilitator will no longer be needed. Often teams become self-facilitating, or the team leader assumes the role of the facilitator.

Adviser. Too often in business, improvement activities and teamwork are simply allowed to happen, but there is not sufficient support for the organization to become a world-class competitor. The executives and managers must be proactive in their leadership role, and this includes improvement activities and establishing teamwork.

Effective teams begin with active leadership support, perhaps from a single supervisor or manager who sees the need for a team activity, such as an improvement team or work cell or from a steering council that determines the need. In either case, the leadership responsibilities are to develop a draft vision statement for the team with preliminary goals and to assign a team leader and a facilitator. Leadership must work with the team leader to ensure that the resources necessary to accomplish the vision are available, and they must clear the organization paths for action when necessary.

A manager or supervisor who establishes a team has a vested interest in its success. Accordingly, this person talks with the team leader from time to time to determine how the team is progressing and to provide guidance and ensure that required resources are available. When a steering council establishes a team, it is desirable to assign one of its members as a senior adviser to the team. This individual has a stake in the team as well as organization experience and clout.

Team Activities

Team activities are the actions the team performs before, during, and after meetings. They can be divided into three parts: preparation, process, and results.

Team Preparations. Team preparation activities need to be accomplished to establish your leadership team, train the team, and prepare for team meetings so the meetings are successful. That means:

- Ensuring that the vision, goals, and objectives of the team support those of the leader
- Selecting the right team members
- Training the team members
- Developing sound plans of action and milestones
- Obtaining the resources necessary for achieving the goals and objectives of the team

In determining the membership of the team, perhaps with the assistance of a facilitator or adviser, review your vision statement and determine the functions needed. Once you have developed a preliminary team membership list, meet with each candidate member and enlist his or her support and participation.

Once the team members are selected, review the list of candidate team members, their past experience in team activities, and their training in the team process and related skills and knowledge. Based on this evaluation, you and the facilitator may agree on a plan for training the team. Training in all cases should be just-in-time training; the team should receive only the training it needs to perform the tasks at hand. Eventually all team members, facilitators, and team leaders will have the needed skills, but this is not practical or even desired in the beginning. Remember that all training has a half-life; if it isn't used, it decays.

At the first team meeting, with everyone in attendance, the team members are introduced to one another and to the team process. Ground rules are established regarding attendance, schedules for meetings, how assignments will be handled, and participation. Training is also discussed and scheduled as appropriate.

After these administrative matters have been completed, the first order of business for the team is to review the vision statement and goals assigned to them. Then they develop the scope for the team, which addresses the time frame for the team, the specifics of the individual goals and objectives, details about the authority of the team to make changes, and completion criteria. Management tools such as affinity diagrams are effective and efficient for planning and provide a good record of the team's planning actions. It is imperative that the vision statement, goals, and scope for the team be documented to ensure a common understanding among all of the team members.

The vision statement, goals, and scope are then used to develop the team's plan of action and milestone chart (POA&M)—the action the team members will be taking. The team must next determine the resources it will need to accomplish its tasks. All of these details must be well documented and accountability needs to be assigned for all activities. Exhibit 4-1 presents a team planning sheet that can be used to organize the team and to communicate its mission, goals, and accomplishments. They cover the information that we have found necessary for planning team activities we have guided, led, facilitated, or participated in.

Next, the team leader and facilitator meet with the manager, supervisor, or steering council that established the team to review the team's vision statement, goals, scope, and POA&M. Periodically thereafter, the team leader meets with the manager, supervisor, or steering council to assess the team's progress, discuss resource requirements, and request leadership assistance as needed. Additionally, the entity that established the team should meet periodically with it to discuss progress, demonstrate leadership interest, and recognize the contributions of the team members to the success of the vision.

Team Process. At this stage, the POA&M is implemented. Each team performs according to its own POA&M, and the specific activities are unique for that team and the subject process(es). Nevertheless, there are some general activities:

▲ *Record keeping.* Record keeping, the administrative aspect of the team's responsibilities, is very important. We recommend that the team leader maintain a master file for the team that

Exhibit 4-1. Team planning summary sheet.

Team Name: _____   Date: _____

1. Team Members:

List each team member and indicate if he or she is a Team Leader (L), Facilitator (F), or Senior Adviser (S).

2. Mission Statement:

Provide a brief mission statement for the team. This addresses why the team exists and may refer to the process and/or problem(s) to be addressed.

3. Goal(s):

List the goal(s) established by this team. If they are "TBD," indicate that in this space and refer to the schedule, which would then include "establishing goals" as one of the tasks.

4. Method(s) of Measuring Success:

List the metrics established by this team. If they are "TBD," indicate that in this space and refer to the schedule, which would then include "determining metrics" as one of the tasks.

5. Completion Criteria:

List the completion criteria for each goal identified. This is where you establish the products and/or services that must be generated for this team to perform its mission.

6. Achievements:

List actual accomplishments, relative to each goal listed in #3 above.

Note: Attach continuation sheets if necessary.

typically contains copies of meeting agendas and minutes; written vision statement, goals, and objectives; team planning sheets (POA&M); action logs; copies of all presentations; and copies of all supporting documentation, including data and charts.

These data are vital for reviewing the progress of the team, developing presentations about the team, retracing steps, educating others about the team, and reviewing decisions.

In the early stages of the team, it is advisable to discuss record keeping in order to develop consensus about what is needed and who will maintain the material. You may want to designate a team member as a permanent scribe, to take minutes, publish meeting agendas, and keep action logs, or you may want to rotate the job among all the members. In either case, this is a critical job on the team and needs to be addressed promptly.

▲ *Process definition.* Regardless of the type of team or its vision, the implementation of the POA&M begins with a process definition: a statement that defines and describes the process assigned to the team. This may be obvious for a team that has been established to develop a work cell, solve a problem, or exploit an improvement opportunity. A team focusing on policies, guidelines, or planning also must develop a process definition.

▲ *Data collection and analysis.* After the process is defined, the team determines what information it needs to refine its POA&M and to accomplish its goals. It collects the appropriate data and performs data analysis.

▲ *Determination of courses of action.* The results of the data analysis are used to derive conclusions and to determine courses of action, recommendations, and corrective actions. At this point, the team is taking direct action to achieve its goals.

Team Results. There is a tendency to focus exclusively on the results of a team activity by measuring the return on investment in order to justify the investment in resources. This focus can be a fatal pitfall. Effective leaders understand that teamwork is a balance of preparation, process, and results. Certainly it is important to measure results, to report them, and to celebrate them as appropriate. Results keep us motivated and reassured that our investments in time and money are worthwhile.

As the team implements its POA&M, therefore, it needs to measure its results to determine if it is accomplishing the expected results, their magnitude, whether they are permanent, and what the future expectations are for the process(es) affected. The answers to these questions are best determined by the customers, internal or external, of the team and the processes affected.

The company leadership needs to recognize the results of the team efforts by honoring the team members and sharing with them the taste of success. When you honor a team, focus on the key values that its members embody in their efforts. Give them public and visible recognition. Some companies have ceremonies or annual recognition days; others have luncheons with the boss. There are numerous variations that you can implement. The message is to do something, and make it personal. All of these ideas, easy to implement and inexpensive, are very well received by employees and greatly appreciated. They will contribute significantly to your efforts to develop a sense of ownership by all of the employees.

Team Phases

Each team passes through four stages or phases as it matures. We call them forming, storming, norming, and performing. The time it takes to get through each phase varies from team to team, as does the intensity of each phase. The better you prepare for your leadership team, the easier it will be to get through the phases.

> *Your leadership team will go through four team phases. The better your leadership preparation and planning are, the sooner you will be performing.*

Forming

The forming stage of a team is a time when the team members first come together. Team members may be unsure of their own role in the team, the role of other team members, or the pecking order of the team. During this tentative time, you as the team leader must guide the members from their status as individuals to becoming team members.

Initially team members are learning acceptable group behavior. There may be some excitement and optimism about the team but also some uncertainty and cautiousness. They are getting acquainted and struggling with the transition to their new roles. It is also common for members to test your leadership and that of the adviser or facilitator.

During the forming stage, each team member will:

▲ Come aboard with great optimism, excitement at meeting the other team members, and anticipation at tackling the vision.
▲ Display great pride in being selected as a team member.
▲ Meet the other team members and feel comfortable being part of the team.
▲ Have some anxiety about the task ahead of meeting the goals and objectives to achieve the leadership vision and concern that the other team members may not have what it takes to keep on track.

Planning is the key during team forming. Good, detailed planning will lay out the tasks, times, and schedules clearly. Members' fears can be significantly reduced with effective communication concerning these schedules, times, goals, and the qualifications of other team members.

The agenda for the first few meetings will cover the following points:

▲ Defining and redefining the goals and objectives to fit the comfort zone of the concerned team members.
▲ Testing of everyone in the team structure. (How do I deal with problems, real and perceived? Can I have a tantrum

or become very authoritarian? Is the best way to make my point forcefully with facts or with emotion?)

- ▲ Constantly expanding and then limiting the information needed to make decisions.
- ▲ Apparently endless discussion about often abstract concepts and principles that may not relate to the goals and objectives of the team.
- ▲ Paper walls, problems and symptoms of problems that are not relevant to accomplishing the goals and objectives or achieving the vision, and difficulty in identifying truly relevant problems.

During this phase, you will accomplish little toward the team's goals and objectives. You can minimize any difficulties by good, detailed planning, clear and comprehensible goals and objectives, and with your leadership skills.

This phase usually lasts from one to three team meetings.

Storming

During the storming phase, your team members may resemble a pack of fighting, snarling wolves more than a group of adult professionals. It is at this stage that many teams fail, and the leadership vision is abandoned. If this occurs, it is because you allow it to occur. Instead, be prepared.

This is a very difficult stage to work through. It is characterized by impatience at the lack of progress, arguing, defensiveness, accusations, and competition among members or groups of members of the team. The team can even break down into cliques, one group against the other.

During the storming stage, your team members will experience:

- ▲ Resistance with using any approach different from that which the team member is accustomed to. ("I've never heard of doing such a thing.")
- ▲ Highs and lows in morale, with attitudes fluctuating rapidly concerning the failure or success of achieving the

vision. ("I don't see how it will ever be possible to do that.")
- Constant arguing for the sake of arguing. ("I agree with you, but I'll be damned if I'm going to do that!")
- Skepticism at the possibility of achieving the vision, goals, and objectives you selected and disbelief at your selection of team members. ("I just don't believe you could have done that!")

Here is your real challenge as a leader. Notice that each of the example statements begins with *I*. This is not necessarily because your team members are self-centered but because they are uncertain about their position, role, or responsibilities. The more the storming continues, the more likely it is that team members will feel threatened and react in this way.

You must clearly and definitively be in charge of these next few meetings, setting the tone, direction, and focus of the discussions. This is best accomplished by:

- Setting and keeping to the meeting agenda
- Continuously focusing on the vision, goals, and objectives without being distracted by side issues
- Remaining uninvolved in the storming, keeping your focus, and staying in control of yourself and your emotions
- Keeping all conversations to the point and professional
- Insisting that every team member hear out other members without interruption
- Allowing each team member time to talk and giving each member the opportunity to reply
- Going around the table in order to each team member to make sure that everything is clear and understood
- Speaking in direct sentences that focus on the positive aspects of the meeting, the team members, and your leadership vision

Rest assured that the team will pass through this phase and come out of it stronger and more capable. Handling this phase properly will gain you the respect of all the team members, who will begin to understand one another and start to think of them-selves as a team.

Norming

In the norming phase team members reconcile their differences with each other and with competing loyalties and responsibili-ties. You are accepted as the leader because of your competence during the storming phase. Conflict within the team ebbs as members become more cooperative and less competitive. The leadership team members realize that they are not going to lose but will win as members of the team. During the norming stage your team members will go through the following phases:

- ▲ Accepting that they are functioning members of the team
- ▲ Realizing that the other team members are, after all, qual-ified contributing members of the team
- ▲ Finding the ability to express criticism in a constructive way through positive statements, not personal attacks
- ▲ Understanding that the vision, goals, and objectives are achievable

Now that the conflict has been reduced and the members accept the team norms, they start to make significant progress toward the team goals. As team members become more at ease with each other and can rationally discuss the team's dynamics, a sense of cohesion grows, and a common spirit at the meetings develops. Your efforts as a leader are paying off the team is func-tioning, and the meeting ground rules are observed.

Performing

At the performing stage, the team is up and functioning and working to achieve the vision, goals, and objectives. The team members have become a cohesive unit, working in concert. They understand the team process and accept and appreciate individ-ual differences.

The team is able to make progress on all the goals and ob-jectives and feel close to each other in their uniform effort. This is the time you too can feel the rewards of leadership. But do not rest. Each time you change the structure of the team, you start over 1 and repeat all the other phases. The duration of the phases will be shortened and the intensity will be lessened, but you will still have to do it again! Additionally your leadership team can fall back into the storming phase from time to time almost cyclically. Be ready, be prepared, and use your principles, traits, and skills.

5

Achieving Your Vision

Establishing your leadership vision is just the beginning. It is the direction you are headed in—a general statement about the future. Many of the details necessary for achieving it are not in the vision statement but will be developed as you define and develop the requisite actions and resources necessary for achieving your vision.

Your leadership vision defines the end point of your journey; your plan defines the path you need to take, so planning is a leadership skill vital to achieving your vision. Other skills are also important, including financial management, marketing, negotiating, and technical skills, but none is so critical to success as planning. Whenever you hear a political, civic, or business leader announce failure, the person never says it was "because of lack of motivation" or "our vision was wrong." The reason is a lack of resources—not enough money or time—or they failed to get their message across to those essential for achieving their vision. These people find themselves halfway to a goal with no more resources because of poor planning and poor implementation of the plan.

Success requires that you have a clear understanding of what it takes to achieve your vision. What resources will you need, what must you do, and how are you going to do it? You need to understand what actions and resources are needed, when you must accomplish each action, how much it costs, and how to get the resources. Then and only then can you make the decision to proceed.

In addition to planning, you need to understand the process for implementing the plan. Here you require project management skills to determine tasking and managing resources.

> *The ability to plan to achieve your vision and to implement your plan, within your budget and on schedule, is critical for achieving your leadership vision.*

Viewing Your Vision as a Project

The tools and techniques for achieving your leadership vision are the same regardless of the magnitude or nature of it, and they are the same tools and techniques used in project management. A project creates a specific result—something you accomplish on your own or with others. Project management is the entire process required to produce a product, a system, or a structure, or it could be a study, a plan, a set of specifications, or software. These products of a project are often called *deliverables*. There is also a set of products associated with achieving your vision: the future situation or condition. These are tangible, measurable results (products) that are required to achieve your vision.

Resources are needed to accomplish a project. One of them is labor—a few individuals or a large number of individuals from many different organizations or companies. Other required resources are materials, equipment, and other items that require expenditures for completing the project.

A project has a life cycle—identifiable starting and ending points that can be associated with a time scale. So does achieving a vision. For a vision the starting point is where you are today; the ending point is where you will be when you have achieved the vision.

The process for achieving your leadership vision includes several distinct phases, and these phases and the skills required for them are the same as those for project management. The interfaces between phases may not be clearly separated. If the vision you seek to achieve is for a sponsor or a customer, formal approval and authorization to proceed are recommended to ensure smooth transition between phases and meet objectives. If the responsibility for achieving the vision is yours alone and you are the sponsor or customer for it, then you are the one to perform the formal approval before starting the next phase. This means that you need to determine where you are headed, evaluate your progress, decide if it is still where you want to go, and make any needed adjustments in your plans and activities.

Just as in project management, uncertainty related to time and cost diminishes as you approach the accomplishment of your vision. This means that as you get closer to your destination, the accuracy of your evaluations increases. The specified result, the time, and the cost to achieve it are inseparable. The uncertainty related to each factor, required for achieving the vision, is reduced with completion of each succeeding phase. The requirements for planning and the control systems capable of predicting the final ending point, as early and accurately as possible, comes directly from this relationship of time, money, and action.

The cost of accelerating the implementation of your plan increases greatly as you approach your vision because there is less time available to speed up your actions. Recovery of lost time becomes increasingly more expensive for each succeeding phase of implementation; also there is less time to speed up your actions, and therefore you need to use more resources. This characteristic of implementation demands integrated control through all phases. You need to be able to assess quickly the impact of delays and changes in the vision and to provide for any adjustments. It is important, therefore, to perform regular, periodic evaluations of your progress.

Achieving your vision involves establishing goals and objectives, determining resource requirements, scheduling, and implementing the plan. This process is the same if you are planning to achieve a personal vision or for an organization vision. For a personal vision—perhaps to become a civic leader or the manager of a department—you may be developing a plan that you will put into action yourself. You are the leader, the team, and the customer for the vision. For an organization vision, you may have a leadership team, followers, and even a customer for the vision. But whatever the case, the concept is the same. It is a process with four phases (Exhibit 5-1).

Phase 1: Defining

The initial vision statement is a general statement about the desired future where you want to go as an individual or as an organization. The statement usually doesn't have any of the details about how you are to achieve it or specifics about the constraints and boundaries for achieving it. The initial challenge for you and your leadership team is to develop a definition of what achieving the vision means. It includes a clear understanding of the purpose, deliverables, constraints, objectives, scope, and strategy for achieving the vision. There needs to be agreement between you and your leadership team about this definition, and if there is an organizational sponsor or customer, it must also be in agreement about this definition.

Two common pitfalls are to move ahead into planning without a complete definition of the vision and without agreement from the organizational sponsor or customer. This is the time to clarify expectations in terms that are meaningful and measurable. Success means achieving your vision on schedule and within budget.

Phase 2: Planning

Effective planning is all of the action needed to achieve your vision. It identifies the resources required for each action and provides a schedule that includes accountability and responsibility. An effective plan is flexible; it provides alternative paths and functions to accommodate changes that may occur during implementation. Changes will occur since the future is unknown, and you cannot control all of the external forces that may affect your ability to accomplish each required action.

The plan for achieving your vision thus consists of the schedule and the resource requirements. Periodically you will

Exhibit 5-1. The four-phase process for achieving a vision.

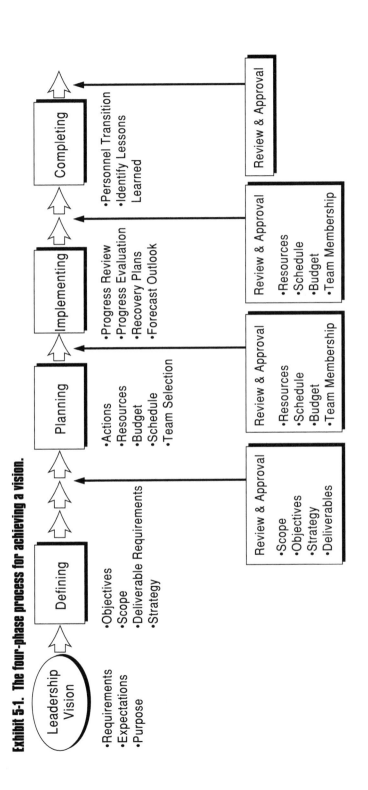

need to review and update the plan to ensure it accurately reflects the progress and activities for achieving the vision.

Phase 3: Implementing

Achieving your vision is the controlled execution of your plan. As the leader you are responsible for coordinating all elements of the implementation of the plan. Each activity needs to be identified and communicated in writing to the performing individual or organization. Progress needs to be monitored and evaluated. Feedback needs to be provided to performing individuals and organizations. Resources need to be obtained and conflicts reconciled.

Achieving your vision is accomplished by understanding what needs to be done and ensuring that capable individuals do this work. This means continuous attention to details, evaluation of progress, and adjusting actions to accommodate changes and delays.

Phase 4: Completing

Your goal is to achieve the vision within the planned budget and on schedule. This means that the sponsor or customer agrees that you have achieved your vision. The completion criteria need to be well defined and documented during the definition of the vision. As changes in your vision or the requirements for achieving it occur, they need to be documented, with the agreement of your leadership team and your sponsor or customer, if applicable.

You will need to plan for the future after the vision is achieved so you know what to do next. You will also need to determine the disposition of the resources used during the accomplishment of the vision. Are they still needed? If not, what do you do with them?

This final step also includes an evaluation of how the implementation of the plan went. This review will identify what went well, and what did not, information that can be used to set better leadership visions and plan for and achieve them.

> *Achieving your vision is similar to managing a project. It encompasses establishing goals and objectives, determining resource requirements, scheduling, and implementing the plan.*

Defining the Vision

To define your vision is to specify details that explain exactly what the situation is when you have achieved your vision—that is, the expectations and requirements of the vision. After you have established the definition, the next step is to determine what you need to do to satisfy those expectations and requirements. This is a list of actions needed to achieve your vision. Thus, a complete definition of your vision will be a list of requirements and expectations and the associated actions needed to satisfy them.

We will use a decision matrix to assist in defining your vision and establishing the goals and objectives that will be used for developing your plan. This matrix will ensure that you identify all of the actions required and provide a method for evaluating them and prioritizing them. In the matrix, a goal is *what* is to be achieved, and the objectives are *how* the goal is to be achieved. In this sense, the vision statement is a primary goal, and the requirements and expectations are secondary goals (Exhibit 5-2).

In the matrix, we list the vision and its requirements and expectations (goals) on the vertical axis, and the objectives on the horizontal axis as the actions to satisfy the requirements and expectations. The individuals responsible for the objectives will need to expand these into defined tasks.

After you have defined the vision, evaluate how each action supports each of the requirements and expectations. We use a visual method to indicate how well each action supports the requirements and expectations and then assign a numerical value for each assessment. The totals in the rows and columns can be used to prioritize your actions and to determine if you

Exhibit 5-2. A decision matrix.

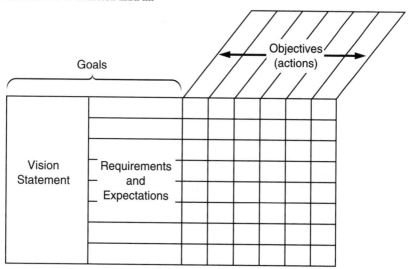

have sufficiently defined the actions needed for achieving your leadership vision.

The completed decision matrix in Exhibit 5-3 reveals many interesting facts about this leader's approach to becoming a recognized leader in his chosen profession. The column totals show the relative weight for each action in support of all the requirements and expectations of the vision. The row totals show how strongly each expectation and requirement is accounted for by the actions. A low total does not mean that an activity or requirement is unimportant; it just reflects its impact relative to the others. This can be a very valuable analysis technique for evaluating the adequacy of the plan and determining the priority of actions.

In the example, our prospective leader has learned several interesting facts. First, the actions do not provide for getting postgraduate training, an omission that needs to be corrected before completing the planning. Second, getting a position with an industry leader and passing state certification do not have as much impact on achieving the vision as the other actions. Our leader may decide that he could accept a position with a small company that would give him broader experience, and he might

Exhibit 5-3. A completed decision matrix.

Legend:
Strong = ● = 9
Medium = ○ = 3
Weak = △ = 1
None = Blank = 0

Vision Statement

Become a recognized leader in my chosen profession

Requirements and Expectations	Get position with leader in industry.	Pass state certification test.	Work in all aspects of chosen profession.	Write articles for professional periodicals.	Implement plan to build leadership skills.	Implement plan for leadership position in professional organization.	Total
15 year's experience at the journeyman level	●	△	○	○		○	19
Skilled public speaker					●	○	12
Skilled team builder and coach			○		●	○	15
Postgraduate training							0
Professional certification	△	●	○	○			16
Published author	△	○	●	●			22
Leadership position in professional organization	△	△	●	○	●	●	32
Total	12	14	27	27	27	18	

consider pursuing postgraduate studies in lieu of state certification. Note also that only two activities contribute to becoming a skilled public speaker. Since this is such an important skill for a leader, he may want to reconsider the actions.

When you develop your own decision matrix, you will be faced with similar situations. This is your opportunity to refine your ideas about your vision and what it means to achieve it. You can also use this information to analyze the impact each action has on the others. When you have finished your decision matrix, each action is then used to determine what must be done in order to accomplish it and the other actions as well.

The goals are what you want to accomplish, and the objectives are how the goals are achieved. In this way you start with a Level 1 goal and develop Level 1 objectives. The Level 1 objectives become Level 2 goals, and so on, to the third level. See Exhibit 5-4, which shows the so-called matrix waterfall.

> *The decision matrix is an important tool. The "what-how" matrix relationship is the characteristic that gives the power to this tool. This relationship generates a family of matrices in a matrix waterfall fashion.*

Defining your leadership vision in preparation for developing the plan uses all of the information collected in developing the vision. The definition of the vision includes the specific details of what it means to have achieved the vision: the set of deliverables or products that are generated and the completion criteria that indicate that you have indeed accomplished your goal and achieved your vision.

The initial steps in defining the vision are these:

- ▲ Defining what it means to achieve your vision
- ▲ Defining the goals for the vision
- ▲ Establishing the purpose for achieving the vision
- ▲ Determining the scope of the vision

Exhibit 5-4. Waterfall of matrices.

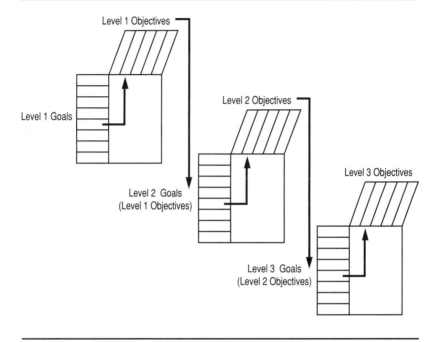

Note: Goals are what are to be achieved and objectives are how the goals are to be achieved.

▲ Describing the completion criteria for the vision (what has to be accomplished)

The clear identification of the completion criteria and specific goals is critical for achieving the leadership vision. As the leader, you need to guide your team in defining the vision so that everyone understands the completion requirements and the goals. Agreement among you, your team, and the organization sponsor or customer at the beginning of this phase will eliminate many potential misunderstandings as well as opportunities for confusion.

The scope is the breadth and depth of the plan for achieving the vision and the constraints as well. It defines your authority and responsibility and establishes the boundaries for your imagination in developing how you will achieve your vision.

Deliverables

The purpose of a vision is to create a future condition. There are specific measurable actions and results that must occur to achieve it—for example, getting an advanced degree; accumulating specific experiences; producing products, services, or information; or a combination of deliverables. These deliverables are the completion requirements that need to be accomplished.

If you have a personal leadership vision, you need to believe it is important and achievable. If it is an organization vision, it is imperative that the organization sponsor or customer and the team agree on the deliverable. Each deliverable needs to be specified in terms of requirements and expectations, with sufficient detail so that the required tasks can be defined, priced, and scheduled, with the required resources allocated for them.

Clear definition of the deliverables also enables the team to establish the completion criteria and to identify all implementation needs up front, thus minimizing planning problems and resource allocation conflicts.

Goals

The goals that you establish for the vision are the things that need to be done to achieve the vision that are not deliverables. They need to be established within the constraints of the vision—what can be realistically accomplished. They also need to be consistent with values. When you establish these goals, they need to be:

▲ *Specific.* Everyone involved in achieving the vision needs to know what the deliverables are. When the goals are vague or not clearly communicated to everyone, they may be interpreted differently. Differences in interpretation may lead to team members' working at cross purposes and will invariably lead to inaccurate planning. The degree of detail needed to specify the goals will vary with the vision. For example, the goals needed for becoming a civic leader do not need to be as detailed as those for becoming a board-certified surgeon or for meeting a sales target of $10 million.

▲ *Timely.* This time element is important for scheduling and ensures that each goal is timely for achieving the purpose of the vision. The time relationships between goals are also important. The timeliness helps establish priorities and urgency for the tasks necessary for achieving the goals.

▲ *Achievable.* Desire is not enough. You and your team members need to believe that the goals are achievable within the constraints of the resources and technology and can be measured to document achievement. Remember that what gets measured gets done.

▲ *Realistic.* The goals for achieving the vision need to be attainable within the constraints of the existing technology and resources. Some say that whatever the human mind can conceive, it can achieve. We believe that what the human mind can conceive *and* believe is possible can be achieved. If the team doesn't believe it can be done, it won't get done.

Thinking in terms of deliverables leads to product-focused goals. The challenge is to identify all the items, including those that are not directly tied to the end product of the vision. These are the ones that often are forgotten until they become a crisis.

Items to consider in setting goals include the following:

- ▲ Purpose
- ▲ Schedule
- ▲ Budget
- ▲ Testing
- ▲ Training
- ▲ Acceptance criteria
- ▲ Risk analysis
- ▲ Quality requirements
- ▲ Facility requirements
- ▲ Logistics

Purpose

Clearly define the purpose for achieving the vision. This statement sets the tone for the tasks ahead and establishes the priority and urgency for the team. A clear statement of purpose sets out what you and your team is doing is important.

Scope

The scope defines the limits and boundaries for achieving the vision. It establishes the authority levels and extent of responsibilities and communicates your limits and your reach. It specifies the requirements and expectations for achieving the vision. Background information needs to be included so that the requirements for achieving the vision can be accurately understood. The scope thus needs to include:

- ▲ Boundaries of authority
- ▲ Level of responsibility
- ▲ Schedule requirements
- ▲ General planning information
- ▲ Equipment requirements or constraints
- ▲ Facility requirements or limitations
- ▲ Documentation requirements

Strategy

After you and your team determine the deliverables and establish the goals and the scope, you are ready to select a course of action for achieving the vision. The strategy for achieving the vision outlines your general approach. Here are the steps for selecting the strategy:

1. List the requirements and expectations for the end result—the vision. What outcomes must be present to be successful? What outcomes are not necessary but would increase satisfaction in achieving the vision?

2. List the goals for achieving the vision.
3. Brainstorm alternative strategies for achieving the goals.
4. Establish strategy evaluation criteria (e.g., constraints in terms of technology, schedule, or resources).
5. Evaluate and prioritize the alternative strategies.
6. Choose a strategy.

Progress Evaluations

Regular, periodic status reports and evaluations are essential for success. During each phase, actions need to be planned, responsibility assigned, and metrics established for each task. As you review progress and evaluate performance, you can develop recovery plans for tasks behind schedule and assess needs for future performance.

Regular, periodic reviews with the organization sponsor or customer ensure that they are aware of your progress. These reviews are also critical to prevent surprises late in the process when problems or delays occur, and they reinforce the importance of the vision and the urgency associated with it.

Vision definition approval is an important element in achieving the leadership vision. There must be agreement among the team members and the sponsor or customers who need to approve the definition. Approval signifies agreement at all levels for the deliverables, requirements, expectations, and scope.

> *The definition of the vision includes the specific details of what it means to have achieved it.*

Planning to Achieve the Vision

A detailed plan is required to achieve the goals of your leadership vision. It specifies tasks to be accomplished, defines all the resources that will be used, schedules for activities, and sets a budget. The plan is critical for managing the tasks necessary for achieving the vision. It serves as the guide for what needs to be done, by whom, when, and with what resources. It is the gauge that progress is measured and evaluated against and the structure for defining the work that needs to be accomplished.

Planning Tools

The decision matrix presented earlier in the chapter provides a good understanding of all the tasks to be performed and their relationship to each other and to achieving your leadership vision. To see how these elements fit together, visualize them as a tree. The roots of the tree are the basic skills, traits, and principles of leadership. The trunk and branches are the specific skills. The leaves are the goals and objectives you must accomplish, and the top of the tree is your leadership vision (Exhibit 5-5).

This analogy leads us to the tree diagram, a tool that is very helpful to you in understanding the structure of how you must build your leadership plans and also provides the basis for another important tool that will assist you in estimating the resources you will require to achieve your leadership vision. The tree diagram is a systematic approach to linking all of the key factors in a plan and linking those factors together in a rational sequence.

Just as your leadership vision is at the top of the tree, so the tree diagram begins with your leadership vision. The tree diagram then breaks the overall vision into subelements of goals, objectives, and skills (Exhibit 5-6).

The development of the tree diagram follows a logical flow. It begins with the leadership vision statement and proceeds in logical sequence to lower and lower goals and objectives, each lower lever adding detail to the tree diagram until the diagram describes specific activities. The finished diagram will give you a strong concept of what you have to do and the sequence you need to accomplish your goals and objectives in.

The tree diagram is defined at as many levels as necessary to provide the proper level of detail for planning. The level of detail you must consider is the level at which you can assess

Exhibit 5-5. The elements of the vision as a tree diagram.

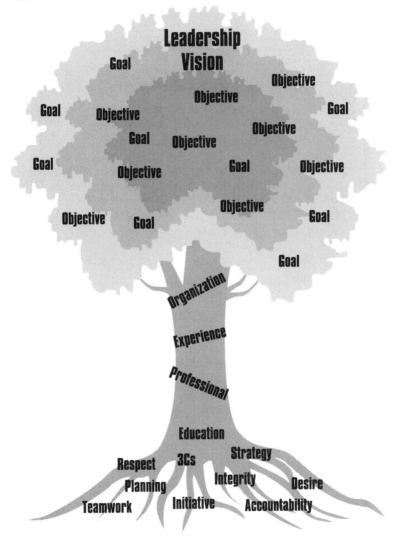

Exhibit 5-6. Leadership tree diagram.

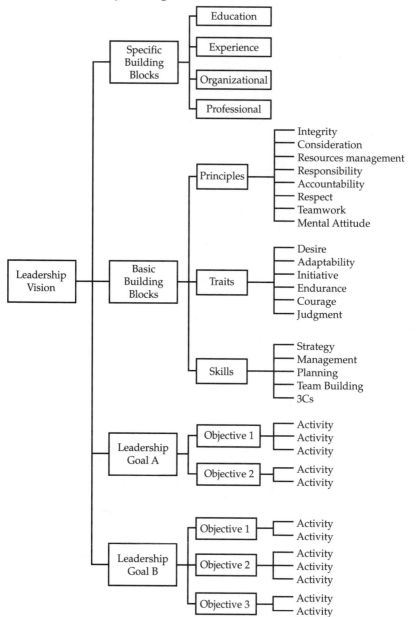

work activities and measure the resources that will be required for you to achieve that goal, objective, or work activity. A detailed breakout of a typical leadership goal to achieve a leadership vision is provided in Exhibit 5-7.

The tree diagram breaks down the work you must accomplish into small, manageable elements and provides a framework for controlling goals, objectives, and work activities; defining personal, organization, and followers' responsibility, authority, and accountability; and measuring and evaluating progress. It forms the basis for developing schedules and cost estimates and assigning resources.

> *The tree diagram is a graphic representation of the project that shows the relationship between product and tasks. As a planning tool, it breaks down the task of achieving the vision into manageable pieces.*

The tree diagram demonstrated in the exhibits is clearly a hierarchy chart with the leadership vision at the top and the lower-level tasks broken down into goals, objectives, and work activities. This process is repeated until the lowest level is reached: the individual activities and actions that can be assigned and performed. This top-down approach is used to guide planning instead of allowing detailed plans to be generated without a common framework. The tree diagram describes

> *A detailed plan is required to achieve the goals for meeting your leadership vision. The plan specifies tasks to be accomplished, schedules for project activities, and budget and defines the resources needed to accomplish the project.*

Exhibit 5-7. A typical leadership tree diagram.

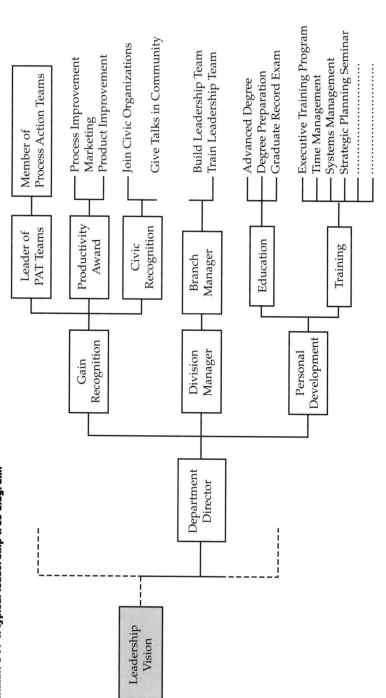

and establishes the required networks and makes the complete process comprehensible at every level of complexity.

Scheduling and Resources

Schedules and resource estimates are important for achieving your leadership vision. A schedule is a written list of actions (in sequence) with dates or times for accomplishing all of the goals, objectives, and preparation required to achieve your vision. This schedule is also used to determine the resources needed to accomplish your vision and thus the cost of the project. Resources are usually viewed as cost/budget, facilities, equipment, people, and time. There are two distinct types of resources to be considered in achieving your leadership vision: (1) personal resources that you must provide for such things as education, personnel changes, and your time and (2) organization costs. Will your organization support training and possibly organization changes to support achieving your vision?

Your schedule for becoming a leader can flow directly from the tree diagram. This is also true of assessing the resources you will need. Scheduling is a critical planning activity since many of the actions will be interrelated and dependent on completion of some other activities before they can begin. The scheduling will also determine when resources are needed to be committed and dedicated for critical activities and will provide the timetable. In order to establish the schedule for achieving your vision, you need to consider:

- ▲ When the vision needs to be achieved
- ▲ What actions are required
- ▲ How long the project will take
- ▲ What resources are needed
- ▲ Where the activity will be done
- ▲ What the prerequisites are for the tasks
- ▲ What the priority is of tasks, goals, objectives, and preparation

Among the many tools for scheduling and estimating resources, we will look at one of the most common and easiest to use: the milestone chart. This tool provides a method for planning, tracking, and controlling the tasks you must perform and can also be used to determine the resources that will be required as well as when they will be required.

The milestone chart is a special bar chart geared to planning and accomplishing activities. Milestones are points in time—usually the beginning or end of an activity. Every individual action in achieving your leadership vision could be a milestone.

All milestone charts are basically constructed in the same way. The top of the chart represents time—the calendar for achieving your leadership vision. This calendar can be in any time period: days, weeks, months, quarters, or years. The left side of the chart lists the activities to be accomplished and their specific milestones, and the schedule for accomplishing each milestone is indicated across the horizontal axis of the chart.

In Exhibit 5-8, the white bars represent current and future planned activities. These are the planned tasks and actions and the estimated time to complete them. The darkened bars represent tasks that have been accomplished. In the same way, the triangles represent planned and achieved milestones. In this example all the tasks have been completed on the scheduled date, a fortunate situation that is not very common.

A milestone chart can be used as well to estimate the resources required to achieve your vision. It will give you an estimate for the total resources required as well as an incremental estimate based on the time you have selected for your milestone chart (weeks, months, etc.). Exhibit 5-9 is a milestone chart for estimating resources using the goals, objectives, and activities from Exhibit 5-8.

This completed milestone chart, with the resources estimates, highlights one of the critical reasons for performing scheduling and resource estimating. It shows that the individual desiring to become a department director must spend an estimated 1,980 hours of time in addition to routine work hours. The individual will also be responsible for costs of $12,000 for obtaining the advanced degree required for consideration as a department head and will have to acquire training from their organization that costs $8,200.

Exhibit 5-8. Milestone chart.

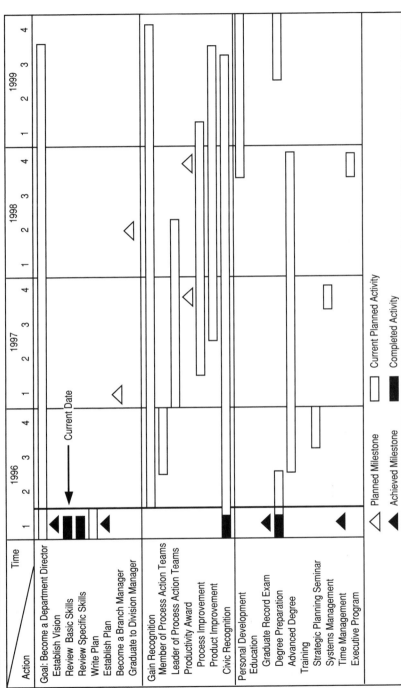

Exhibit 5-9. Milestone chart with resource estimates.

Action \ Time	1996				1997				1998				1999			
	1	2	3	4	1	2	3	4	1	2	3	4	1	2	3	4
Goal: Become a Department Director																
Establish Vision	▲															
Review Basic Skills ← Current Date	■															
Review Specific Skills	■															
Write Plan	□															
Establish Plan	▲															
Become a Branch Manager					△											
Graduate to Division Manager										△						
Gain Recognition																
Member of Process Action Teams																
Leader of Process Action Teams																
Productivity Award							△				△					
Process Improvement																
Product Improvement																
Civic Recognition	■															
Personal Development																
Education																
Graduate Record Exam	▲															
Degree Preparation	■															
Advanced Degree																
Training																
Strategic Planning Seminar																
Systems Management						□										
Time Management	▲															
Executive Program										□						

Resources	1	2	3	4	1	2	3	4	1	2	3	4	1	2	3	4
Budget (Personal)		$1,200	$1,200	$1,200	$1,200	$1,200	$1,200	$1,200	$1,200	$1,200	$1,200					
Budget (Organization)			$1,500				$980				$5,800					
Time (Extra Hours)	30	30	180	180	180	180	180	180	180	180	180	180	30	30	30	30

Total Personal Budget $12,000   Total Organization Budget $8,280   Total Additional Personal Time 1,980 hours

Review and Approval

The written plan for achieving your vision will vary in size and complexity depending on the size and complexity of the vision. It will specify the deliverables, objectives, schedule, cost estimates, resource requirements, and project controls.

Once the plan is completed and agreed on by the team members, it is reviewed for agreement and approval by the organization sponsor or customer. If it is a personal leadership vision, you are the customer and the sponsor and thus the approval authority.

> *Scheduling—deciding when work will be performed—is a critical activity since many of the actions will be interrelated and dependent on completion of some other activities before they can begin. The scheduling will also determine when resources are needed to be committed and dedicated for critical activities.*

Implementing the Plan

Developing a plan is a large task that requires a lot of attention to detail because it will be the guide for all that you do to achieve your vision. Many leaders are unsuccessful even when they have a good plan because they fall short in its execution. They either do not delegate well or do not review and develop recovery plans for slips. The key to success in this phase is regular review of progress, with identification of problem areas and the development and implementation of recovery plans.

In this phase you coordinate all the elements of the project of achieving the leadership vision:

- ▲ Controlling work in progress
- ▲ Providing feedback to those performing the actions
- ▲ Negotiating for resources

- ▲ Resolving conflicts
- ▲ Developing recovery plans
- ▲ Forecasting

Implementing begins with written task statements for each activity that specify deliverables and associated task performance standards in terms of schedule, cost, and performance. Each activity will have a performance plan and budget that can be reviewed and evaluated for performance.

> *Review. Review. Review.*

Communication is key to successful implementation. Any problems or changes need to be communicated to all the team members and the organization sponsor or customer as soon as possible so the team can work together to solve problems with a minimum impact on the schedule and budget.

Implementing the plan requires constant review and evaluation of progress. As progress is made and changes occur, the plan needs to be revised. This analysis will provide early identification of schedule and budget problems. When these occur it is imperative that the team develop and execute recovery plans to get back on plan.

Progress reports are necessary to ensure that all key individuals are informed of the status of the project. The progress reports include a summary of progress for the reporting period, milestones schedules, recovery plans, and project outlook.

Completing the Process

Completing is the final phase of the process of achieving your vision. This marks your arrival at the destination you have set for you and your team. You will need to prepare for this phase just as you have for the others by these activities:

▲ Recognizing that the completion criteria have been accomplished.
▲ Celebrating your arrival at your vision.
▲ Determining what to do next. Do you set a new vision? Does your team continue with you or move on to other activities?

During this phase be sure to capture the lessons learned for future activities—for example:

▲ Major problem areas and their solutions
▲ New or improved management techniques
▲ Suppliers who performed particularly well
▲ Recommendations for future actions

> *Achieving your vision is the beginning of a new future. It is time to celebrate your arrival and time to set a new vision for a new future.*

6

Understanding and Overcoming Resistance

Communication, cooperation, and coordination are the three strategies that you as a leader will need to win over your leadership team, gain followers, and overcome resistance, overt or covert, to your leadership.

The 3Cs: Communication, Cooperation, and Coordination

The most effective method of dealing with potential resistance to leadership is through communication, cooperation, and coordination—the 3Cs of achieving your leadership vision. This method of communicating, gaining followers, and countering resistance is the most effective path to achieving your vision because it frequently eliminates resistance before it starts.

> *The 3Cs is the best method for you to gain adherence to your leadership vision and overcome any potential resistance.*

Communication

Communication is defined in the broadest sense here as the transmission of meaning to others. In leadership it has two distinct components: formal communication—the dissemination of information through some specific medium, written or electronic—and informal communication—which transmits much more than words. By its nature, personal communications also transmit nonverbal messages—your feelings, motives, and attitudes. In interpersonal communications, your expressions, attitude, tone of voice, and body language transmit much more than your words do.

There is a relationship among the words you use, the symbols of your leadership, and your nonverbal communications. These three relationships form a triangle of effective communication. All three corners of the triangle must be in concert for your communication to be effective (Exhibit 6-1).

At the top of the triangle are the words you use; they are the basis for your communication. What you say orally or in writing is the beginning of your communication, but only the beginning. These words must communicate your meaning directly and clearly. You must say what you mean and mean what you say.

The symbols you use to communicate—logos, banners, slo-

Exhibit 6-1. The components of effective communication and their interrelationship.

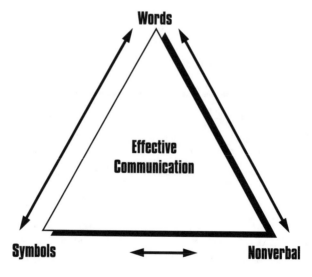

gans, and graphics—can be powerful tools in communicating your thoughts and meaning. They must be in concert with what you are trying to communicate, or they may negate your words. Someone standing under a banner that reads, "PEOPLE ARE OUR MOST IMPORTANT ASSET" and then stating that he is laying off thousands of employees will not be taken very seriously.

Nonverbal communications—body language, attitude, and expressions—matter very much in communicating your real thoughts. An executive at a board meeting can ask a simple question, "Does any board member have a problem with this program?" If she speaks with an expression of concern and makes direct eye contact with the board members, she will elicit responses. The same sentence spoken with a scowl and a steely-eyed glare will receive no response.

If you cannot communicate effectively, you cannot lead. It is crucial to communicate effectively and frequently with everyone involved early in the leadership process. This is a process of one-on-one discussions, presentations to organizations and groups, and communication by every medium possible.

The best form of communication is a clearly defined and formally stated goal. The vision and goals stated for effecting leadership must be clearly consistent with the goals and objectives of the followers. The need for change and the logic leading to a change decision should be outlined, explained, and documented. This documentation transforms the needed change from your idea to a reality. Finally, for maximum effectiveness, a broad dissemination of all the factors affecting leadership is necessary.

> _To lead, you must communicate effectively._

Leadership communication is a dialogue because one-way communication does not work. Anyone can give directions; that is simply the process of managing and supervising, not leading. Leadership requires effective communication that is a two-way dialogue. That dialogue consists of five specific forms of communication: personal communication, written and electronic communication, meetings, presentations, and organization communication.

There are a few basic rules of communication that apply to all communication media:

- ▲ Communicate clearly, whether verbally, in writing, or electronically. Avoid using questions or allegories that obscure a point.
- ▲ Communicate directly. Do not use abstractions to disguise direct statements.
- ▲ Be brief. Do not use long anecdotes and unwieldy examples.
- ▲ Use active listening. Reflect each communication back to the speaker until you both are clear on the meaning. Be sure not to debate each statement.
- ▲ Do not conduct a running commentary as others are speaking.
- ▲ Share information on many levels of understanding.

Personal Communication. Personal communication is the daily one-on-one communication that occurs in your organization: providing direction, asking and answering questions, listening to your followers' concerns, and so forth. To your leadership team, this can be a motivating experience or a distressing one. This experience carries over into all other aspects of achieving your vision. If it is negative, it will inhibit the accomplishment of your leadership vision. If it is positive, it will be a motivating factor and will lay the groundwork for your leadership. First and foremost you must be able to communicate personally with the members of your leadership team and the others in your organization.

The key to successful individual communication is dialogue: open two-way communication, that is, listening and talking. This is a personal exchange. Every time you have an individual communication with one of your team members, followers, or employees it should be a personal discussion. That person should come away form that conversation with the strong feeling that you were talking to him or her personally, listening closely. There are a number of barriers to individual communication:

- You are not present.
- You are not listening.
- You are making assumptions or premature evaluations.
- You are playing one-upmanship.
- You are hostile or negative.
- You do not have control of the situation.

The word *you* appears in every one of these barriers to communication. This means that you as a leader have to be responsible for the quality of each and every communication. Following are a few guidelines for effective personal communications:

- *Be there.* When having a personal communication, do not appear to be preoccupied with other thoughts. Rather, give that person your undivided attention. Talk directly to the person, and use his or her name. Your body language communicates as well. Do not let it give the impression that you do not want to be there.

- *Listen.* Be an active listener. Paraphrase key points made by the other person and reflect them back to the individual. Verify your understanding of the person's statements, feelings, and facts by asking relevant questions and linking the statements together into statements of fact or specific actions. This kind of listening requires effort, but the reward is a very effective communication.

- *Consider new ideas.* Do not make assumptions before the other person has finished talking. Never (NEVER) cut the other person short or interrupt until he or she has finished, or you will inhibit, if not immediately stop, any effective communication. Hold your evaluation until you have clearly demonstrated that you comprehend the idea and understand the facts. Whenever an idea is being presented to you, take time to listen, consider, and answer in positive terms, even if you are turning down the proposal.

- *Be "we-win" oriented.* Make very conversation a winning conversation. Do not play one-upmanship with your team members, followers, or employees. This game is juvenile and wearisome and diminishes your position and stature as a leader. Do not trap yourself in an I win–you lose mode of thought. Remember that your objective is to win as a leader and achieve your leadership vision, not win every point of every discussion.

▲ *Be positive.* If you appear threatened and distressed by any new or opposing view, your team members and employees will be reluctant to discuss anything with you in the future. They will find another leader who is not hostile or negative to every input. Try to understand others' views. When a new idea is appropriate, accept it. If it is not appropriate give due credit to the individual for the effort and thought, and be clear why the idea cannot be incorporated.

▲ *Communicate clearly.* Plan and organize your thoughts so you think before you speak. Speak in clear, concise sentences using the language of the listener. Strive mightily for clarity through active listening. To lead, you need to be understood.

▲ *Manage conflict.* You must be willing to confront conflict, an integral part of being a leader. Conflict will come, and it will come to you. Never deny another person's conflicting views, pretending that they do not exist or are irrelevant. Face it, and then manage, minimize, and channel it into positive directions by dealing with it on a factual basis. You cannot resolve conflict with opinions or hyperbole. You *can* resolve it with facts.

Written and Electronic Communication. As a leader you are expected to be an effective writer in various forms: memorandums, formal reports, letters, meeting minutes, proposals, and e-mail. (Notice that we left e-mail for last. Today a glut of information is available through electronic media. Some leaders sit before their monitors all day sending instructions and asking questions on e-mail and believe they are leading or managing an organization through that exchange. Electronic systems can be effective communication tools, but they are just that—tools—and not substitutes for personal communications.)

Written communication in some ways is more difficult than the spoken word; since you are not present, your attitude, body language, and expressions cannot be read or interpreted by the reader. Nevertheless, the focus of this form of communication is the same: an effective communication that results in understanding and action. This requires that you put yourself in the place of your audience and write to their needs, then visualize what their likely reaction will be to your written communication. Your writing should be as alive as if you were addressing another person in an animated conversation.

Following are some common barriers to effective written and electronic communication:

- Lack of clarity
- Lack of focus
- Lack of coherence
- Improper language for the audience
- Dull and boring presentation
- Not to the point

You can overcome them by using simple and direct rules:

- *Employ commonalty of language.* This means writing to your audience's education level, experience, and interests. Before you begin writing, think about your reader and visualize how your communication will be received. Remember that it is you who desire to communicate. Write so that your audience can clearly understand your ideas, thoughts, and concerns. Remember the simple rules of good grammar. Write in short, declarative sentences that are not open to misinterpretation, and avoid clouding the issue with unnecessary verbiage. Write good lead sentences to each paragraph and several supporting sentences. Be sure the paragraphs are supportive of the focus of your communication.

- *Focus on the key issues.* Organize your document to support this idea or fact. Whether the written communication is a one-page memo or a forty-five-page report, maintain your focus. Write so that the document supports the central theme of your correspondence. Develop other ideas as secondary and in support of your main idea.

- *Write coherently.* Organize your material to tell a story from beginning to end. Do not inject new ideas in the middle of a paragraph or in the middle of several paragraphs discussing a single subject. In each paragraph, the first sentence should state a specific idea or question, with the following two to four sentences supporting that idea or amplifying on it. Similarly, your lead paragraph will introduce your theme and the following paragraphs will support it. Here too short declarative sentences communicate best. Following is a step-by-step guide to writing your document:

1. Write a clear, concise theme or subject as the lead sentence and the lead paragraph.
2. Present the relevant data or information concerning the subject.
3. Discuss the relevant facts and the data in detail. Make no assumptions about the reader's knowledge.
4. Draw conclusions based on the data and discussion. You cannot draw conclusions about data or information you have not discussed.
5. Make recommendations. You cannot make recommendation for which you have not drawn conclusions.

▲ *Use clear language.* Your writing style will have an impact on the reader, so select your style with the reader in mind and follow it throughout the communication. Examples of styles are formal business style, speaking in the first person, using scientific descriptions and notation, and conversational tone. Always use the active voice rather than the passive voice, and select the shortest and most commonly used words because they are most effective and carry your ideas furthest.

Meetings. Much of your leadership team's work will be accomplished in meetings. Team members, followers, and employees will carry out assignments and perform many tasks between meetings; it is during meetings that discussions occur, decisions are made, and actions are decided upon. Conducting productive meetings can be quite difficult since few leaders and fewer team members, followers, or employees know and understand the skills needed. The best way to have a productive meeting is to understand the barriers and rules to conducting good meetings. Some of the barriers are:

▲ Lack of focus
▲ Poorly defined purpose
▲ Lack of agenda control
▲ No closure
▲ No follow-up

The key to conducting a productive meeting is to follow these guidelines:

▲ *Always have an agenda.* This is true of *all* meetings, even ad hoc meetings of only a few people. Take a moment to establish an agenda and define why you are meeting, what you hope to accomplish, and how long it should take. Once you have an agenda, stick to it to keep the meeting on track. Agendas should include:

— *Specific agenda items:* the topics that will be discussed at the meeting. Items should be presented in a short sentence or phrase, with an agenda item for each subject of discussion.
— *Presenters of the topics:* usually the person who requested the item be added to the agenda. That person will come to the meeting prepared to present and discuss the item.
— *Time frames for presentation and discussion:* specific start and end times of the meeting, with each agenda item allotted time for presentation and discussion.
— *Identification of type of presentation for discussion, information, or decision:* decision agenda items, which require action. They are usually preceded by information presentations, or a point paper is provided to the team members before the meeting. Never make a cold decision presentation at a leadership meeting.

▲ *Be clear about the purpose.* When you have taken the time to schedule a meeting, you should have a very clear idea of why you are all there. Meetings should be conducted when you have a problem to solve, you have a decision to make, you need to inform or be informed. Before asking for a meeting, determine what the outcome should be. That is your purpose for meeting.

That you always have a meeting on Friday at 2:00 is *never* a good reason.

▲ *Encourage participation by all meeting attendees.* Do not ask people to come to a meeting if you do not expect or want them to participate. To encourage participation, call on them individually if necessary, and ask for an opinion. Be prepared for disagreement. (If this were easy, you probably wouldn't need a meeting to discuss it.) Listen to the participants and process their information.

▲ *Always summarize at the end of the meeting.* Give the participants a sense of closure—that this was a good meeting and accomplished its goals. Clearly define decisions that have been made and action items assigned and selected. Be sure that everyone understands their action items and that they appear in the minutes of the meeting.

▲ *If a meeting is worth having, it is worth writing minutes.* Minutes are the written record of your meeting that set out agreements, decisions, and actions. Having this information in writing will prevent misunderstandings. These minutes should include:

— The time, location, and purpose of the meeting
— Names of all attendees
— Names of presenters
— The subjects presented and discussed
— The decisions made and actions assigned
— The scheduled time and location of the next meeting and known agenda items
— A request for the attendees to review the minutes, correct inaccuracies, recommend changes, and add agenda items for the next meeting

Presentations. Leaders must be dynamic and effective public speakers. In many situations you will be called upon to speak before a large group and deliver a presentation. These presentations will give you significant public exposure and the chance to have an impact on others.

There are some barriers to being an effective public speaker.

Just like many of the other barriers to leadership, they can be overcome with education, practice, and personal discipline. The most common barriers to effective public speaking are:

- *Lack of preparation.* This occurs when you are not totally familiar with your subject or with the material you are going to present.
- *Canned talks.* The same talk or speech given over and over again or the presentation that you have memorized puts audiences to sleep.
- *Failure to speak to your audience.* This is the "you people" syndrome. Do not talk over the heads of your audience or look and sound disinterested in them.
- *Poor visual aids.*
- *Too much material in too little time.*

The key to effective public speaking is focusing not on covering the material or reading a canned script but on having a dialogue with your audience. The following simple rules will greatly assist you in making effective presentations:

- *Be prepared.* This is a cliché but very true. Carefully research and prepare your materials, and prepare yourself on them by reviewing the information until you know it. Be sure that your material is authentic and that your visual aids are ready and correct. Know your audience too—their educational, technical, and professional level. And try to determine if they have any agendas concerning the material you are about to present. Finally, be flexible. You may well be surprised by the size and makeup of your audience. Perhaps you prepare for a formal presentation with transparencies or slides, but it becomes clear that your audience would rather sit down and discuss the subject. Do not get flustered in this situation. Remember that this is your material and your subject, and you can present it in any way you see fit.
- *State your purpose.* Clearly define the purpose of your presentation: what you want the listeners to get from it. Organize your material, your visual aids, and your thoughts around a central purpose or theme. Understand if your presentation is:

— Educational or training
— Information only
— A decision brief
— Asking your audience to do something
— Asking your audience to believe something
— Trying to inform, train, or educate your audience

▲ *Speak from an outline, never a script.* It is always a mistake to memorize or read your talk. Your audience will lose interest and maybe even doze a bit while you are droning on in a monotone presentation. Instead, use an outline that you glance at occasionally, and deliver your talk directly to the audience with passion. Impart that this is a subject of interest and importance to you, and you feel strongly about it.

▲ *Speak directly to the audience*—not over their heads, not at their feet, not to the podium. Speaking to the audience is one of the most important traits of a successful public speaker. Look at the audience and individuals in it. Hold their eye contact for several seconds or long enough to make a point. This is a captivating trait, and one that you can learn. As you speak, move about and gesture as appropriate. Get excited about your subject, and the audience will also. One caution: This will work only if you are authentic. If you are talking from a script or are insincere about the subject, your acting will show.

Organization Communications. As a leader, communication is the tool you use to carry out all of your organization functions: planning, organizing, staffing and staff development, directing and leading, and evaluation and controlling. Communication is your most important tool. Here are some barriers associated with organization communication:

▲ Failure to communicate the mission and goals of the organization
▲ Failure to communicate where the organization is going and how it plans to get there
▲ Failure to provide your team, followers, or employees with the information they need to carry out their jobs.
▲ Failure to provide accurate and timely feedback

These impediments underlie many leadership, business, and organization problems, such as lack of leadership credibility and lack of trust. The resolution of these impediments could transform an enterprise in trouble into a successful one. Following are guidelines for achieving effective organization communication.

▲ *Frequently communicate your leadership direction.* Let everyone know where the vision, goals, and objectives are headed. This is especially important during times of change.

▲ *Inform everyone about the major leadership issues that are influencing the organization.* A leadership proactive approach will be far more effective than a reactive approach. Rather than being placed in a defensive position of reacting to various rumors about specific issues, leaders should take the initiative in establishing an ongoing program that periodically informs everyone about the issues of the day and what is being done to resolve them.

▲ *Provide information to your followers frequently.* Providing accurate and complete information to everyone is a principal way of achieving trust and getting the job done. It is your responsibility as a leader.

▲ *Lead by walking around.* This is not a new concept, but it is indispensable to organization communication. A significant portion of your workweek should be devoted to interacting with your followers on a one-to-one basis. This is organization communication at its best. Nothing can replace it.

> *No matter how intelligent or innovative you are or how important your position is, these qualities are of no use if you cannot communicate your ideas effectively.*

Cooperation

Cooperation, the second of the 3Cs, is the act or instance of people working and acting together for a common purpose or benefit. It will be necessary for your leadership team to be cooperative for more than an instant if you are to be successful. Cooperation needs to become a way of life for you, your leadership team, and your followers.

A deeper look at the nature of cooperation will reveal why people do not cooperate. Often there is no reward for not cooperating, and there may well not be any consequence for not cooperating. Moreover, the rewards for being cooperative may be tentative and undefined.

Some leaders are the biggest block to cooperation. If they talk about cooperation and insist on it yet pass out rewards based on individual competitive results, cooperation will not be a hallmark of their team. You as the leader must implement a win-win attitude toward cooperation and avoid fostering an I win–you lose atmosphere among your leadership team, followers, or employees.

Directly involving potential resisters to your leadership in the design and implementation of change can forestall resistance. Form a network of those potential resisters because they may have something positive to contribute. This strategy is practical if those individuals can perceive some benefit from your leadership or can limit the negative effects of the change on them personally. It is not very practical to involve them if they are potential net losers in the change process.

In the spirit of cooperation, display some flexibility. Be prepared to compromise with your network, and do not expect 100 percent acceptance.

There are known barriers to achieving cooperation among your leadership team, followers, or employees:

- ▲ No reward system for cooperation
- ▲ A competitive environment
- ▲ Little trust
- ▲ No commitment to change

A few basic rules of cooperation will help overcome the natural resistance to it:

- ▲ *Network those affected.* As you implement your leadership vision, changes affecting people will necessarily be made. Networking those affected, and integrating them into your change process, is an effective way of overcoming potential resistance. Make them part of the team or give them specific responsibilities in achieving your leadership vision. If they participate in achieving your vision, it is difficult for them to resist your leadership.

▲ *Be prepared to compromise.* Compromise is a basic rule of cooperation. When working with your team or networking those affected by your leadership, promote compromise along the way.

▲ *Instill a commitment to cooperate.* This is done first by removing the incentives for your leadership team members to be competitive with each other. (There will still be plenty of competition with outside forces.) The leadership team or your organization as whole should be cooperating to win—to achieve your leadership vision. Provide incentives for cooperation; reward team efforts and minimize individual rewards.

Coordination

Coordination, the last of the 3Cs, is the active interaction of functions or elements of a system for a common purpose. This definition is close to that of cooperation; indeed, the two functions are closely related.

A well-coordinated leadership effort can help deal with resistance by being supportive of the elements required to implement change. This process includes providing the support needed to facilitate your leadership changes among the individuals and elements of the organization; providing the training and education necessary to implement new skills and standards; planning and structuring the change so that it can be effectively transitional; and executing the planned change rather than just allowing it to happen in a haphazard way.

Some barriers to coordination are:

- ▲ Poor lines of communication between team members
- ▲ Conflicting support requirements among such diverse activities as facilities management, finance, transportation, and writing issues

▲ Assumptions and/or outdated information being provided to and/or used by team members

▲ Failure to document (in writing) complex plans or schedules

Many of these barriers to coordination can be overcome
with good planning and attention to detail on the part of the
leader. Communication also plays a vital role in coordination;
the leader, as the catalyst in the dissemination of information,
must communicate frequently with the team.

A 3C program can be very effective when any resistance is
based on inadequate information or incomplete data. The program facilitates the change agent's acquisition of help from all
employees, including potential resisters. It fosters good relationships between the change agent and the resisters. The program
requires time and effort, however, and it will not negate all resistance to change. The change will always have a negative effect
on some individuals and parts of an organization.

Utilizing the 3Cs will win you the most adherents to your
leadership and eliminate most of the resistance. Nevertheless,
inevitably there will be resistance. You must understand the
causes of it and be prepared with techniques to overcome it.

Resistance to Your Leadership

All leaders—business managers, supervisors, civic leaders, pol-
iticians, or employees—encounter resistance, a natural response
to any change. If you are competing to win a leadership position, you are surely proposing change. Experienced leaders are
aware of this fact, yet rarely do they perform a systematic analysis to determine who might resist and for what reasons.

To anticipate what form resistance might take, leaders need
to understand its most common causes:

▲ *Narrow-minded motivation.* There are always individuals in
any organization who are very narrowly motivated; self-
interest is their only motivator.

▲ *Lack of understanding and confidence.* Some individuals have a distinct lack of understanding of what needs to be accomplished and why. On the basis of past experience, their confidence in the organization or individual may be low. This lack of confidence leads to mistrust and resistance.

▲ *Different analysis of leadership needs.* Based on the information available or the information you have provided, some people in your organization may have a completely different assessment of the needs for leadership and change.

▲ *Low tolerance for change.* This type of resistance usually comes from employees who feel they cannot cope with the change required.

Each of these causes has distinct motivations and must be understood. Once you have this knowledge, you can determine which of these causes apply to your situation and use that knowledge to counter the resistance.

Narrow-Minded Motivation

The fear of losing something of value—position, salary, or status—is always a motivation to resist change. Self-interest causes people to consider first their personal situations and not that of the organization. The following changes can be expected to result in resistance:

▲ *Changes that alter an individual's status*—for example, changes in level of authority (real or perceived), salary or salary status, or title

▲ *Changes that reduce decision-making power*—for example, reducing the scope of someone's responsibilities, centralizing decision making, or using team consensus to make decisions

▲ *Changes that interfere with existing relationships*—for example, moving individuals outside their existing network or moving employees or supervisors

People often attempt to subvert new leadership before and during planning and implementation if they do not view the proposed change as personally beneficial. The resistance is rarely open. Instead, subtle approaches are used and tend to occur beneath the surface, using back channels of communication.

Many individuals in an organization are in positions to resist your leadership in this way:

- ▲ The financial manager who just cannot release the funds at this time
- ▲ The shop foreman who stops operations daily for safety hazards but who offers no preventive action
- ▲ The administrative assistant who frequently calls in sick at critical times
- ▲ The planning coordinator who never seems to return your phone calls
- ▲ Individual team members who never offer opinions or suggestions

Lack of Understanding and Confidence

Individuals and groups may resist your leadership if they do not understand its implications and if they perceive that it will cost them more than they will gain. These situations occur most often where there is a lack of trust between the individual initiating the change and the employees. Rarely is there a high level of trust among executives, managers, supervisors, and employees. Unless clear and precise communication, cooperation, and coordination accompany change, misunderstandings surface when the following types of change are introduced:

- ▲ Changes in individual status that are not clearly defined
- ▲ Changes that require a level of trust between the change agent and individuals
- ▲ Changes that have been poorly communicated and coordinated

Misunderstandings must be recognized and resolved rapidly, for if they are not addressed, they often lead to resistance.

Different Analysis of the Situation

Commonly, people resist leadership change when they evaluate the situation differently from you. Assumptions are the damaging elements here. Frequently those initiating change assume that they have all the relevant data necessary to conduct a thorough analysis and that everyone else in the organization is working with the same data. This problem arises when:

- ▲ Change data and information are not thoroughly disseminated
- ▲ Evaluation of change data is performed using different methods
- ▲ Assumptions leading to the need for change are not clear

Low Tolerance for Change

People resist change because they fear that they will not be able to cope with the new skills and behavior that will be required. Organization changes sometimes require people to adapt more rapidly than they are able. These are the changes that may lead to conflict:

- ▲ Changes that require skills beyond the individual's perceived capabilities
- ▲ Changes that are beyond the training and education of individuals
- ▲ Changes that are beyond an individual's ability to absorb
- ▲ Changes implying that previous actions and decisions were incorrect

Resistance stemming from limited tolerance is emotional, even when the change is clearly in the individual's and the organization's best interest. This low tolerance also surfaces when individual egos are threatened by a belief that the change is an admission that previous decisions and methods were wrong.

Overcoming Resistance: The Strategies

To implement your leadership fully, it is necessary to overcome resistance. As you do, you will achieve a transition from traditional leadership and management methods to world-class leadership.

You will have several strategies at your disposal: the 3C approach, always the most successful and desirable; negotiating and agreement, a strategy used in many environments that can be successfully implemented; and manipulation, the least desirable, which will provide only short-term gains. If none of these works, termination may be in order.

Achieving your leadership vision is always characterized by skillful leadership in the application of a combination of approaches that best fit your situation. Most successful efforts are based on approaches with a sensitivity to your strengths and limitations and a realistic appraisal of the situation. The most common mistake leaders make is to use only one approach or a limited set of them, regardless of the situation. Typical examples are the hard-boiled boss who often coerces people, the people-oriented leader who constantly tries to be (over) involved, and the cynic who always manipulates and co-opts. The point is that leadership cannot be confined to a single principle. The best approach fits the situation.

The most desirable strategy is communication, cooperation, and coordination. Use it first, and you will achieve a large part of your leadership vision. Based on your assessment of the situation, you may need to negotiate and reach agreement with some elements of your organization. This strategy will become necessary when dealing with people in a strong position or in a union environment. Finally, there is the Prince Machiavelli strategy of manipulation and coercion—the least desirable strategy and one to turn to only after very careful consideration and as a last resort. Employment of this leadership strategy always leads to difficulty and eventually erodes your leadership position. (Exhibit 6-2 compares these strategies.)

A second common mistake that managers make is to approach change in an unstructured way rather than as part of a clearly considered strategy. The approaches to change and the

Exhibit 6-2. Strategies for overcoming resistance: a comparison.

Strategy	Situation	Strengths	Limitations
3Cs: (Communicate, cooperate, communicate)	Leadership based on correct information and data	Creates leadership advocates and change agents; very positive attitude of the followers	Requires significant time and effort, including the expertise to communicate
Negotiation and agreement	Leadership based on individual benefits for the followers	Easy way to avoid major resistance; creates followers motivated by need	Can be expensive and time-consuming
Manipulation and co-optation	When other tactics will not work or are too expensive	Relatively quick and inexpensive	Will lead to future problems with personnel; never a long-term solution

urgency for its implementation indicate the change strategy for countering the resistance.

The greater the anticipated resistance is to your leadership, the more difficult it will be to overcome. This is especially true in industrial organizations or bureaucracies with entrenched resisters. Your leadership approach depends on four basic factors:

1. *The amount and kind of resistance you anticipated.* If resistance is strong, it may be necessary to move down the strategy list. The application of good negotiation skills is always helpful here.

2. *Your position with respect to the potential resisters.* If you are in a strong position, the 3C approach will always work best.

3. *The availability of relevant data.* If there is an excellent, well-documented basis for leadership change, the 3C approach will work best.

4. *The stakes.* Higher stakes for you and your organization may require you to move down the list to manipulation and co-opting.

Implications for Leaders

All of the strategies have implications for leaders. To determine what they are and how they will affect your efforts, conduct an analysis of the factors relevant to producing the needed change. This analysis focuses on the potential resistance to change:

- Determining how and where within an organization each of the methods for leadership needs to be applied
- Selecting a leadership strategy and specifying where on the strategic continuum the strategy will lie
- Monitoring the process and adjusting as necessary

No matter how well you plan your initial strategy and tactics, something unexpected will occur. It is always necessary to adjust the strategy and methods as the change process progresses.

You can significantly improve your chances of success in any change effort by following these guidelines:

- Conducting an organization analysis
- Evaluating the factors relevant to producing the needed change
- Selecting the methods to be applied
- Selecting a change strategy
- Monitoring the implementation process

Communication skills are a key to this method, but not even the most outstanding leadership will make up for a poor choice of strategy, lack of planning, or ineffectively applied methods for overcoming resistance. In a world that is becoming more and more dynamic, the consequences of poor leadership will become increasingly severe.

Negotiation and Agreement

Offering incentives to potential followers is a way to achieve your leadership vision and is frequently used throughout industry. Needed changes in work rules, benefits, and productivity can be balanced with higher wages, early retirement, and production incentives. Negotiation is an effective way of dealing with change when there is clearly someone who will lose and that individual or group has the power to resist. It can also be time-consuming and expensive.

Manipulation and Co-Opting

Manipulation and the selective use of information can be an effective way to deal with resistance. Co-opting an individual or group usually involves giving that person or group a role in the design or implementation of change. This is not a form of participation, however, because you do not want the participation of the person co-opted, merely his or her passive endorsement.

Co-opting can be a relatively easy and inexpensive way to gain an individual's or group's support, and it is cheaper than negotiation, but there are some drawbacks. If individuals and groups feel they are being tricked into following, are not being treated equally, or are being lied to, they often respond in a very aggressive and negative way. Another serious drawback to manipulation and co-opting is that if you develop a reputation as a manipulator, it will undermine your ability to use better approaches such as the 3Cs method. Use co-opting when other strategies have not worked or change is urgent, and there is insufficient time to implement the first two strategies.

Termination

After all of these efforts have been made to overcome resistance, there may still be some individuals who refuse to accept you as a leader. This is where the least desirable and final solution must be used: termination. You cannot allow a single individual to stop you from achieving your leadership vision and affect your whole organization negatively.

The best strategy to avoid and overcome resistance is of course the 3Cs. Communication, cooperation, and coordination are the firm foundation on which you can build in order to avoid moving down the list of strategies to the last and least desirable.

7

The Leadership Challenge

The challenge in all leadership environments today is in the transformation from management and entitlement to leadership. With the ability to lead effectively, you can identify and make decisions related to your activity, to achieve your leadership vision. In industry we can no longer be sustained by superior technology and productivity alone. All business enterprises must cope with an evolving environment in which diverse workforces, changing business needs, disparate locations, and changing markets must be brought together.

Your Personal Challenge

All leadership starts with personal leadership. You first must lead yourself to accomplish your personal leadership vision. Recall the building blocks of leadership set out in Chapter 1, and understand that these traits, principles, and skills form the foundation of your leadership. The basic leadership skills are laid upon a strong foundation of leadership traits and the leadership traits rest on a foundation of principles.

Achieving your leadership vision must be a structured process that begins with your knowing and understanding your personal values. What is it that you truly want? How will leadership help you achieve it? Then you must understand the basic requirements of leadership—the principles, traits, and skills that you must have to achieve your vision. These building blocks must be realistically assessed and adjustments made to your capabilities and character where required.

The next step is to create your leadership team. Carefully select and nurture it, for participation will not occur by itself nor can it be forced. The responsibility and involvement of your team members are the keys. Fully integrate your leadership team into your leadership vision, goals, and objectives. Every team member has collaborative individual goals.

Leadership involves all of the members of your organization, whether they are volunteers, employees, or followers. If your leadership is to be successful, there are ten things you should be prepared to do:

1. Share power and authority.
2. Build mutual trust and respect.
3. Provide training in team building, process analysis, and problem solving.
4. View all tasks as a cooperative undertaking with the participation of your leadership team, management, supervisors, and employees. Be willing to accept consensus decisions, and at the same time be willing to reject solutions that are not beneficial.
5. Be willing to decentralize decision making.
6. Get out of the finger-pointing mode of fault finding. You will learn quickly that progress is much more important than authority.
7. Believe that everyone can have good ideas, and that combining these good ideas into consensus is productive and profitable.
8. Chase fear out of your workplace. The work environment is conducive to developing employee loyalty. That loyalty is a hard currency that is banked, saved, and traded upon, just as cash receivables are.
9. Organized labor is an interactive part of the program and participates in the leadership team.
10. This is a long-term commitment, just as the acceptance of your leadership vision is a strategic decision.

With the implementation of these methods, quality and productivity will be improved, and so will two-way communication. As stronger leader-follower-employee relationships develop, overall morale will improve. Problem solving will occur at all levels of the organization, and problems will be solved before they become priority issues for leadership.

When you become a leader and decide to put together a leadership team, do not assume that everyone—followers, employees, and unions—will be roadblocks. In fact, in case after case, rank-and-file employees and their unions have willingly participated in these programs. Typically it is the people already in a position of power—supervisors and front-line managers—who offer the most resistance, for several reasons: they feel threatened by the loss of authority; they do not understand the leadership vision or its effects; they perceive this as a high-risk activity to them personally; and they are blind to benefits to themselves. You can avoid resistance by the methods we have proposed. Remember when dealing with someone in a position of power, say, supervisors and managers, that they are individuals just like the other employees in the company. Don't dictate leadership to them. First, lead the change by using the 3Cs method and gain their support. The active participation of this level of management is crucial to successful leadership.

You can effectively implement a leadership team by taking the following actions:

- *Educate managers, supervisors, and employees.* Be sure everyone's working from the same plans, with the same tools, and using the same process. Training in the problem-solving and decision-making processes will accomplish this result.
- *Define the structure clearly.* All employees at all levels must understand where they fit in the organization and its structure. They must know what is expected of them and how results will be measured.
- *Implement a system of rewards and corrective action.* Be sure to review reward and corrective action programs very carefully.
- *Get everyone aboard early.* Involve all levels of management and supervision from the beginning.
- *Establish networks.* The most convincing argument for the implementation of your leadership vision is made by

your peer group. Establishing networks that encourage peer groups to review and exchange ideas about your leadership vision is an effective way of convincing others of its value.

- ▲ *Live it.* The best way to convince everyone at all levels of the value of your leadership vision is to become a part of it yourself. Live it. Walk it. Talk it.
- ▲ *Use the domino theory.* As the work-related decision responsibility moves lower and lower in an organization, authority also must move down. This delegation of authority will strengthen the position and prestige of the employees.

Obstacles to Leadership

Experience had taught us that there are two specific roadblocks to achieving your leadership vision, and they both have to do with *you.*

Unwillingness to Confront and Resolve Issues

The first and foremost obstacle you will place before yourself in achieving your leadership vision is an inability or unwillingness to confront and resolve issues. There will always be hard decisions to make concerning finances, priorities, organization performance, and issues associated with inadequate or improper performance by individuals. In many cases, your leadership team, employees, or followers will be more directly and continually affected by these problems than you will. Everyone will have a sense of frustration if you do not confront these issues directly.

Typically these issues are avoided by leaders who like to delegate their resolution to the leadership team members or ignore them altogether. They will not go away, and the longer you ignore them, the more serious and widespread they will become. Your leadership team expects you to lead, especially in tough situations. Resolving issues can be difficult and personally stressful if you let it be, especially if the issues have to do with people and performance. Remember the 3Cs and how you use this principle and the other methods of overcoming resistance; they are of great help in resolving these issues.

The resolution of these issues reflects upon the basic principles of responsibility and integrity and requires courage plus good communication and management skills. As a leader, you must have a well-structured and consistent approach to resolving these problems. A basic four-step approach is:

1. *Define the issue clearly.* In a concise problem statement, focus on the issue, not personalities or perceptions, and determine how it relates to achieving your leadership vision and your values.
2. *Gather all the facts based on the problem statement.* Decide what information is available to you to perform an evaluation and draw a conclusion. Gather this information.
3. *Evaluate the facts compared to the requirements.* Evaluate the facts and consider how they relate to the problem statement. What do these facts say about values, vision, goals, and objectives?
4. *Make a fact-based decision concerning achieving your leadership vision.* Then stand by the decision unless different facts are presented to you. Be firm and resolute.

Diluting Your Leadership Efforts by Lack of Focus

As you move toward achieving your vision, your leadership team must function effectively and efficiently. To accomplish this they must stay focused. A serious leadership failing is to add new action items or even new goals and objectives at every leadership team meeting. This is a natural tendency as information increases and situations change or arise, but the leadership team's efforts become diluted with too many priorities. It is especially damaging to place constant pressure on your team and followers to perform a never-ending list of objectives, action items, and changing priorities, each of which you call critical. Soon the team members become immersed in achieving meeting-to-meeting action items, while the focus of achieving the leadership vision becomes secondary. This problem relates to the basic principle of constancy of purpose, the leadership trait of resolution, and your planning and management skills.

Focus is the key to avoiding this obstacle to leadership. You must be focused upon achieving your leadership vision and understand that secondary issues are just that—secondary. Without strong leadership, focus, and constancy of purpose this can very easily occur.

One of us was once asked to facilitate a leadership team where focus had clearly been lost. The vision—to expand the organization from division level to department level (a growth of 500 percent)—required significant efforts in the growth of organization capability and expanded markets. But the leadership team was far behind in meeting its milestones for achieving this vision. It was currently debating the color of carpeting and style of new furniture for the expanded facilities, caught up in administrative decisions concerning the centralization of financial management and contract management, and spending a lot of time on designing and developing a new employment application. These action items had taken up four biweekly team meetings. The focus of this leadership team had been lost in secondary priorities.

Keeping focused on the vision, goals, and objectives is critical to avoiding this pitfall. As a leader, you must decide on priorities and actions and guide your leadership team. As new priorities, action items, and even goals and objectives present themselves, you must evaluate them in the light of keeping focused on your leadership vision. The best tool to use here is delegation. Not every action that needs to be taken must be accomplished by the leadership team, so delegate those that can be done by subordinates and trust them to come up with the right decision. In the brief example above, the design and development of a personnel form should have been delegated to personnel or human resources and the furniture and facilities decisions to a cognizant leadership team member so the team could return its focus to expanding markets and organizational capabilities.

The Road Map to Leadership

The leadership model presented in this book is intended to provide a road map for potential leaders. It will show you the way to successful leadership and structure your leadership process. Since change is one of the few constants we can be sure of today, you will be reassessing your leadership vision continually and updating the basic skills you will need to remain in a leadership position.

You should now have a crystal-clear understanding of the distinction between managing—directing others—and the process of leading—motivating others to excel. Managers direct the allocation of resources including people; leaders ignite people to perform by knowing, understanding, and implementing the leadership principles, traits, and skills. This structured philosophy is the foundation of all successful leadership.

The leadership self-assessment in Appendix A will show you where you are and where you need to improve or change to be an effective leader. Appendix B contains a leadership plan to be constructed based on your self-assessment. This leadership plan will be your road map to becoming a leader.

You is the key word in achieving your leadership vision. Success as a leader is totally dependent upon *you*—your actions and your achievements:

- ▲ You must have the desire to be a leader.
- ▲ You must have the management skills to be a leader.
- ▲ You must have the technical skills to be a leader.
- ▲ You must have the communication skills to be a leader.
- ▲ You must have the planning skills to be a leader.
- ▲ You must be willing to make personal sacrifices to be a leader.

> *You will be a leader of significant impact if you have the desire and are willing to live by the principles, traits, and skills of leadership.*

Appendix A
Leadership Self-Assessment

This self-assessment is designed to provide a baseline for determining where you are in achieving your leadership vision and where you have to go. The purpose of this assessment is to provide the basis for completing Appendix B, your plan to achieve your leadership vision. You and the members of your leadership team should complete this self-assessment. It will assist you in measuring how far you must go to achieve your vision and what you need to do.

This assessment includes the five elements of the leadership model. Each of these elements is to be measured using a scale of 0 through 100, in increments of 20. For each item, assess your preparation, training, education, knowledge, or ability to lead in that area. Mentally answer each question in a category. Then, on the basis of all your responses, assign yourself a numerical value according to the following scale:

0 = No preparation, education, training, knowledge, or ability

20 = Very slight preparation, education, training, knowledge, or ability

40 = Some preparation, education, training, knowledge, or ability

60 = A working knowledge

80 = A journeyman ability to implement

100 = Total mastery and confidence in this area

You may also wish to utilize the blank diagrams pages 145 to 147 to aid in your self-assessment. These diagrams promote thought about what leadership characteristics you most value.

Record your scores on your leadership profile, which follows:

Your Leadership Profile

Profile	0	20	40	60	80	100
Principles						
Traits						
Skills						
Vision						
Teams						
Communicating						
Achieving						

LEADERSHIP PRINCIPLES

1. Do you make decisions in a timely manner?
2. Are you a self-confident person?
3. Do you have a sense of responsibility?
4. Do you understand and can you describe your basic values?
5. Can you communicate effectively orally and in writing?
6. Are you tactful in dealing with your peers and subordinates?
7. Do you seek responsibility?
8. Are you guided by a clear set of values?
9. Are you able to set the example for your followers?
10. Do you consider yourself competent to fill a leadership position?

Numerical Value _____

LEADERSHIP TRAITS

1. Is your desire to be a leader strong enough to make personal changes and sacrifices?
2. Can you adapt to different situations quickly?
3. Do you have the mental and physical endurance to be a leader?
4. Do you exercise sound judgment in making decisions?
5. Do you have the courage to face difficult situations and difficult people?
6. Do you have the self-confidence to be a leader?
7. Do others have the confidence in you to be a leader?
8. Can you focus yourself, your time, and your resources on becoming a leader?
9. Do you exhibit enthusiasm? Are you enthused about what you do?
10. Do you have the integrity needed to be a leader?

Numerical Value _____

LEADERSHIP SKILLS

1. Do you have the education required to be a leader in your chosen field?
2. Do you have the training necessary to be a leader in your chosen field?
3. Do you have the practical knowledge and experience to be a leader in your chosen field?
4. Do you possess the required financial skills needed to achieve your vision?
5. Do you have the business skills needed to achieve your vision?
6. Do you have the planning skills needed to achieve your vision?
7. Do you have the personal communication skills needed to achieve your vision?
8. Can you effectively network with others in your selected area of leadership to build a supporting structure for your leadership?

9. Do you have the team-building and -facilitating skills you will need?
10. Can you communicate effectively orally and in writing?

Numerical Value _____

LEADERSHIP VISION

1. Do you clearly understand your basic values?
2. Do you clearly understand the basic values of your organization?
3. Do you clearly understand the values of your followers?
4. Do you clearly know and understand your competencies and those of your followers and the organization?
5. Is your vision based on the reality of your underlying values and competencies?
6. Have you achieved consensus about your values and vision with your leadership team?
7. Can your leadership vision capture the imagination and ignite the enthusiasm of your followers?
8. Is your vision based on the financial facts of your business situation?
9. Is your leadership vision achievable?
10. Is your leadership vision collaborative with the needs of you, your followers, and the organization?

Numerical Value _____

LEADERSHIP TEAM

1. Do you know what skills you need in a leadership team?
2. Do you have team members with planning skills?
3. Do you have team members with financial skills?
4. Do you have team members with business skills?
5. Do you have team members with technical skills?
6. Do you actively involve team members in establishing goals and objectives?
7. Do you have a team structure? Have you selected your team members?

8. Do you have a team facilitator?
9. Do you know how to run effective team meetings?
10. Have you determined how you are going to measure team success?

Numerical Value _____

COMMUNICATING

1. Do you understand the natural causes of resistance to your leadership?
2. Do you understand how to use communication to overcome this resistance?
3. Are you effective in individual communication?
4. Can you communicate effectively in writing and electronically?
5. Can you lead effective meetings?
6. Are you an effective public speaker?
7. Can you communicate to your organization effectively?
8. Do you practice active listening?
9. Are your communications brief and to the point?
10. Do you communicate in clear, distinct sentences that can be clearly understood by the listener?

Numerical Value _____

ACHIEVING

1. Do you understand the strengths and limitations of your leadership team?
2. Can you fulfill your team's needs for improvement?
3. Do you have a complete and realistic plan of action and milestones to achieve leadership?
4. Do you know and understand your strengths?
5. Do you know and understand your needs for improvement?
6. Do you have the training and education resources required?
7. Do you have the experience needed to be a successful leader in your chosen field?

8. Do you have the budget available?
9. Do you have the time available?
10. Do you know how you will measure success once it is achieved?

Numerical Value _____

Here is a completed leadership profile that indicates how ready this person is to be a leader. The profile also serves as the basis for completing the leadership plan in Appendix B.

Profile	0	20	40	60	80	100
Principles	███████					
Traits	█████████					
Skills	███████					
Vision	████████████					
Teams	█████					
Communicating	███████					
Achieving	██					

On the basis of his self-assessment, this potential leader knows that:

▲ He has a weak background for achieving his vision.
▲ His vision *itself* is clear and well defined.
▲ Teaming and communication capabilities are low and need some work, possibly through training and education.
▲ Principles, traits, and skills need to be better defined.

In Chapter 3 we described how to evaluate your values to ensure they support all the leadership principles. Following are blank diagrams for use when assessing your personal or organization values compared to the basic leadership principles and traits. The last of these blank diagrams is a relationship matrix for comparing your skills against the leadership skills. The charts are to assist you when you perform your self-assessment to determine if your values support the leadership principles and traits and to determine if you possess the skills necessary to be an effective leader. The results of this analysis are used in the development of your leadership plan of action (see Appendix B).

Your Leadership Vision Statement Leadership Principles Your → Values											T O T A L
1. Integrity											
2. Effective communication											
3. Responsibility, acccountability, authority											
4. Positive mental attitude											
5. Consideration and respect											
6. Constancy of purpose											
7. Teamwork											
8. Effective resources management											
9. Fact-based decision making											
Total											

Your Leadership Vision Statement											T O T A L
Leadership Traits Your ⟶ Values											
1. Controlled emotions											
2. Adaptability											
3. Initiative											
4. Courage											
5. Determination and resolution											
6. Ethical behavior											
7. Sound judgment											
8. Endurance											
9. Desire											
10. Dependability											
Total											

Your Leadership Vision Statement Leadership Skills Your ———→ ↓ Values										T O T A L
1. Team building										
2. Management										
3. Planning										
4. Communication										
5. Coordination										
6. Cooperation										
Total										

Appendix B
Leadership Plan

Having completed the leadership self-assessment, you are now ready to complete your personal leadership plan, which will give you a more precise picture of what you need to accomplish to become a leader and achieve your leadership vision. This will serve as a self-development plan that is closely related to the leadership process discussed in Chapter 1. You must give this plan serious thought and be completely honest with yourself in assessing the answer to each question. You are exercising your own judgment concerning your own leadership strengths and needs. If you are not completely honest, you will only be fooling yourself.

Your leadership plan should be based on the strengths and need for improvement based on your leadership self-assessment. This approach to planning can best be implemented using a management tool such as a milestone chart. The plan will ask you to list your strengths in each leadership element, list your needs for improvement in each leadership element, and provide a plan of action and milestones for accomplishing the needed improvements. You will also list the resources you will need to accomplish this improvement.

LEADERSHIP PRINCIPLES

A. What are your strengths?

_____

_____

_____

_____

_____

_____

B. What are your needs for improvement?

_____

_____

_____

_____

C. Plan of action and milestones

Plan of action _____

_____

_____

Milestones (with start and completion dates): _____

_____

_____

D. Resources required

Training _____

_____

Education _____

_____

Experience _____

_____

Budget _____

_____

Time _____

_____

LEADERSHIP TRAITS

A. What are your strengths?

_____

_____

_____

_____

_____

B. What are your needs for improvement?

_____

_____

_____

_____

_____

C. Plan of action and milestones

Plan of action _____

_____

Milestones (with start and completion dates) _____

_____

_____

D. Resources required

Training _____

_____

Education _____
_____

Experience _____
_____

Budget _____
_____

Time _____
_____

LEADERSHIP SKILLS

A. What are your strengths?

_____
_____
_____
_____
_____

B. What are your needs for improvement?

_____
_____
_____
_____
_____

C. Plan of action and milestones

Plan of action _____

_____

_____

Milestones (with start and completion dates) _____

_____

_____

D. Resources required

Training _____

_____

Education _____

_____

Experience _____

_____

Budget _____

_____

Time _____

_____

LEADERSHIP VISION

A. What is your leadership vision?

_____

_____

_____

_____

_____

B. What are the needs to improve your vision?

_____

_____

_____

_____

_____

C. What plan of action and milestones are needed to convert this vision into reality?

Plan of action _____

_____

_____

Milestones (with start and completion dates) _____

_____

_____

D. Resources required

Training _____

_____

Education _____

_____

Experience _____

_____

Budget _____

_____

Time _____

_____

LEADERSHIP TEAM

A. What are the strengths and limitations of your leadership team?

_____

_____

_____

_____

_____

B. What are your team's needs for improvement?

_____

_____

_____

_____

_____

C. Plan of action and milestones

Plan of action _____

_____

_____

Milestones (with start and completion dates) _____

_____

_____

D. Resources required

Training _____

_____

Education _____

_____

Experience _____

_____

Budget _____

_____

Time _____

_____

COMMUNICATION

A. What are your strengths as a communicator?

_____

_____

_____

_____

_____

B. What are your needs for improvement as a communicator?

_____

_____

_____

_____

_____

_____

C. Plan of action and milestones

Plan of action _____

_____

_____

Milestones (with start and completion dates) _____

_____

_____

D. Resources required

Training _____

_____

Education _____

_____

Experience _____

_____

Budget _____

_____

Time _____

_____

Achieving Your Leadership Vision

A. What are your strengths?

_____

_____

_____

_____

_____

B. What are your needs for improvement?

_____

_____

_____

_____

_____

C. Plan of action and milestones

Plan of action _____

_____

_____

Milestones (with start and completion dates) _____

_____

_____

D. Resources required

Training _____

_____

Education _____

_____

Experience _____

_____

Budget _____

_____

Time _____

_____

E. How will you measure success?

_____

_____

Bibliography

Blank, Warren. *The 9 Natural Laws of Leadership.* New York: AMA-COM, 1995.

Deming, W. Edwards. *Out of the Crises.* Cambridge: Massachusetts Institute of Technology, 1986.

Harrington-Mackin, Deborah. *Keeping the Team Going: A Tool Kit to Renew & Refuel Your Workplace Teams.* New York: AMACOM, 1996.

Harrington-Mackin, Deborah. *The Team Building Tool Kit: Tips, Tactics, and Rules for Effective Workplace Teams.* New York: AMACOM, 1984.

Hudiberg, John J. *Winning With Quality: The FPL Story.* White Plains, N.Y.: Quality Resources, 1991.

Kepner, Charles H., and Trego, Benjamin B. *The New Rational Manager.* Princeton: Kepner Trego, 1981.

Kerzuer, Harold. *Project Management: A Systems Approach to Planning, Scheduling and Controlling.* New York: Van Nostrand Reinhold, 1992.

Koerstenbaum, Peter. *Leadership: The Inner Side of Greatness.* San Francisco: Jossey-Bass, 1991.

Marshall, Edward M. *Transforming the Way We Work: The Power of the Collaborative Workplace.* New York: AMACOM, 1995.

Nanus, Burt. *Visionary Leadership.* San Francisco: Jossey-Bass, 1990.

Orsburn, John D.; Musselwhite, Ed; Zegler, John H.; with Perrin, Craig. *Self-Directed Work Teams: The New American Challenge.* Homewood, Ill.: Dorsey Press, 1990.

Ouchi, William G. *Theory Z.* New York: Avon Books, 1981.

Peters, Tom. *Thriving on Chaos.* New York: Knopf, 1988.

Phillips, Don T. *Lincoln on Leadership: Executive Strategies for Tough Times.* New York: Warner Books, 1992.

ReVelle, Jack B.; Jackson, Harry K.; and Frigon, Normand L. *From Concept to Customer.* New York: Wiley, 1995.

Thurow, Lester. *Head to Head.* New York: William Morrow and Co., 1992.

Tichey, Noel M., and Devaanna, Mary Anne. *The Transformational Leader.* New York: Wiley, 1990.

Tregoe, Benjamin B.; Zimmerman, John W.; Smith, Ronald A.; and Tobia, Peter M. *Vision in Action: Putting a Winning Strategy to Work.* New York: Simon & Schuster, 1990.

Walton, Mary. *The Deming Management Method.* New York: Putnam, 1986.

Weinberg, Gerald M. *Becoming a Technical Leader—An Organic Problem-Solving Approach.* New York: Dorset House Publishing, 1986.

Index